BAR MITZVAH

BAT MITZVAH

we invite you to share

a special day in our lives

as we proudly celebrate

our daughter

alice melanie

עֲלִיזָה חַוָּה

being called to the torah

as a bat mitzvah

❀ ❀ ❀

saturday, the fourth of september, two thousand four

at nine-thirty in the morning

beth tfiloh congregation

baltimore, maryland

ellen and robert keeper

kiddush to follow

BAR MITZVAH

PLANNING THE PERFECT DAY

Amy Nebens

PHOTOGRAPHS BY ELLEN SILVERMAN AND DAVID LEWIS STERNFELD

Stewart, Tabori & Chang
New York

BAT MITZVAH

Text copyright © 2005 Amy Nebens

Photographs by Ellen Silverman, copyright © 2005 Ellen Silverman: pages 2, 7, 11, 19, 22, 37, 40, 43, 47, 50, 51, 60, 63, 64, 67, 69, 77, 81, 86, 89, 98, 99, 100, 101, 103, 104, 106, 109, 112, 115, 117, 121, 125, 133, 141, 144, and jacket: front cover (bottom) and back cover
Photography assistant: Christina Holmes
Stylist: Cindy DiPrima

Photographs by David Lewis Sternfeld, copyright © 2005 David Lewis Sternfeld: pages 18, 24, 31, 34, 35, 48, 55, 70, 110, 116, 122, 126, 134, 136, 137, jacket: front cover (center)

Project editor: Sandra Gilbert
Production manager: Kim Tyner

Published in 2005 by
Stewart, Tabori & Chang
115 West 18th Street
New York, NY 10011
www.abramsbooks.com

Canadian Distribution:
Canadian Manda Group
One Atlantic Avenue, Suite 105
Toronto, Ontario M6K 3E7
Canada

Library of Congress Cataloging-in-Publication Data.
Nebens, Amy M.
Bar Mitzvah : planning the perfect day / Amy Nebens ; photographs by Ellen Silverman and David Lewis Sternfeld.
p. cm.
"Bat mitzvah" — bottom of t.p.
ISBN 1-58479-415-1
1. Bar mitzvah. 2. Bat mitzvah.   I. Title.
BM707.N33 2005
395.2'4 — dc22
2004062609

Designed by Jill Groeber
The text of this book was composed in Interstate and Bulmer.

Printed in China

10 9 8 7 6 5 4 3 2 1

First Printing

Stewart, Tabori & Chang is a subsidiary of

LA MARTINIÈRE
GROUPE

Page 2
Invitations come in all shapes, sizes, colors, and designs. These simple invitations are infused with the day's color scheme: fuschia type is letterpressed onto white paper and used to trim the paper's thick edges. Similar invites using yellow and lime green rest to the side.

Page 7
Bags are a fun, festive, and inexpensive way to package favors. Here clockwise from left: A baseball card is tied onto a blue paper bag; for a winter theme, a snowflake adorns a shiny white bag; a cellophane bag allows guests to see the pretty package inside; candy necklaces are tempting in this mesh bag.

DEDICATION

TO MY WONDERFUL HUSBAND, Edward, who is always my number one fan and TO OUR THREE BEAUTIFUL CHILDREN, whose bar and bat mitzvahs we look forward to planning together one day. TO MY PARENTS, who instilled in me a sense of tradition and made possible my own bat mitzvah memories. AND TO MY BIG SISTER, who let me stay close by her side on her special day and gave me lots of encouragement, support, and love when it came to mine.

ACKNOWLEDGMENTS

This book was the result of the talent, ideas, expertise, and dedication of a number of people. First, I would like to thank Sandy Gilbert, my editor, for her support and guidance as she saw this book tirelessly and patiently through from beginning to end. My gratitude also extends to my agent, Jane Dystel, for her brilliant idea, support, and guidance through this process. To photographer Ellen Silverman, whose pictures wonderfully brought to life the words and ideas. To David Lewis Sternfeld, for his expert advice and for his photos, which infused even more energy onto the pages. To stylist, Cindy DiPrima, whose talent turned our ideas into tangible details. And to designer Jill Groeber, who turned the words, pictures, charts, and more into a book that is a delight to look through. Many thanks also to the people at Stewart, Tabori & Chang—publisher Leslie Stoker, legal advisor Meryl Jacobs, production manager Kim Tyner, art director Galen Smith, and editorial assistant Dervla Kelly.

I would also like to express my gratitude to family and friends who have helped make this project come to be. To my sister and brother-in-law, Joy and Morey Wildes, for their advice, patience, and unending support. To Amy Conway, for her advice and professional opinions. To Catherine Woodard, for opening her home to us. To Aaron Freidus, Peter Jacobs, Perri Blitz, and Hayley Cooper, who eagerly participated in an afternoon photo shoot. To our kid experts: Aaron Freidus, Peter Jacobs, Chloe Richards, Adam Kaplan, and Noah Sheinbaum. And our parent experts: Avis Richards, Rae Kaplan Reyes, Jeff Kaplan, Catherine Woodard, Zeva Oelbaum, and Judy Greenfeld. And to the many professionals for their advice and willingness to lend their expertise to make our book its best.

CONTENTS

INTRODUCTION

It may seem like just yesterday that you brought your new baby home, celebrating the occasion with family and friends at a bris or baby naming. Then, before you knew it, as if life fast-forwarded, a decade flew by and your baby is almost a teenager—with the walk and the talk to prove it—and you're thinking about a bar or bat mitzvah. It may be hard to believe, but the time to begin laying the groundwork for this next milestone is now. There are classes to attend, a ceremony to prepare for, Torah portions to be learned, a celebration to plan, and, of course, memories to be made.

"Bar" or "bat mitzvah," which translates in Hebrew as "son" or "daughter of the commandment," refers to the observance of the Jewish coming of age and is an automatic rite for every Jewish boy or girl—no pomp and circumstance necessary. But who wouldn't want to mark this auspicious day with a special event? There may be no mention of the bar mitzvah ceremony in the Torah, but today there is quite a salute to the occasion. After all, the completion of many years of Hebrew school, religious study, and rigorous bar mitzvah training—as well as the entrance into Jewish adulthood—are cause for much fanfare indeed.

**BABY TO BAR
MITZVAH**
They grow up so fast—
it's almost never too
early to think about
planning and prepar-
ing for your child's bar
or bat mitzvah.

For some families this turning point can also be cause for much anxi-
ety, considering the preparation required for planning an event like
this. But there is little need to worry since the blueprint for the festivities already exists. All bar and bat mitzvahs start with a religious service—most people choose to hold the service in a synagogue, although
some bring the ceremony to a new and different location of their
choice—complete with prayers; Torah portions; special honors, or
aliyot; and more. All this followed by a reception that combines a fun
party with a celebration that recognizes the significance of the day.

This book is a useful tool when planning a bar or bat mitzvah,
whether you have no time to lose or are already thinking years ahead.
Since the key to planning is to be well informed, well organized, and
flexible, each chapter is filled with facts, information, and explanations
as well as expert advice for both the ceremony and the party. The
advice comes from the well-known experts—A-list professionals in
their fields—and the self-made ones—parents and children who have
planned and participated in a bar mitzvah of their own.

You will read about the significance of the bar or bat mitzvah, the services, and the customs and rituals that go along with it. You will find descriptions of the types of services; some differ in length and time of day. You will also learn about the symbolism that is a part of each. And you will gather new ideas of how to personalize yours. You will also learn key logistical details such as when to sign up for religious school training and when to book a synagogue date. And you will come to understand the etiquette and finer points of planning and being host at such an event. Most important, at a time when your child and his or her friends are attending so many bar or bat mitzvahs, this book is also filled with scores of ideas for party venues, themes, catering, entertainment, and more, all to help make your celebration anything but typical. It will introduce new possibilities, offer inspiration, and help you and your child brainstorm some wonderful ideas of your own.

Throughout these pages you will also find advice, tips, checklists, and worksheets. Focus on the timeline and the budget planner first. Stay organized with checklists for topics such as stationery and photography and with the guest list worksheet. Refer to glossaries scattered throughout the book on Hebrew terms, printing styles for stationery, and photography details, just to name a few. Look for idea boxes for party themes, favors, and entertainment. Get tips and advice on everything from religious training and ceremony responsibilities, to making the party both kid and adult friendly, to finding the right party professionals, to understanding contracts. Explore new ideas for prayers, speeches, menus, favors, decorations, themes, invitations, and more. And, in the following chapters, notice that we move back and forth between using bar and bat mitzvah, he and she, son and daughter, because *Planning the Perfect Day* is meant for everyone.

Not only will this book become an invaluable guide for you, but it will also be helpful in discussing the occasion with your child. You will find it is a wonderful way to foster communication from the start—and remember that your child's opinion is of utmost importance since kids do make up a generous part of the guest list, and it is your child's day in the spotlight. Who better to lend insight to that? Perhaps best of all, if the event is a collaborative effort that includes the whole family, you can enjoy the planning and preparation almost as much as the day itself. And you can bet your guests will too.

1

FIRST THINGS FIRST

IN THIS CHAPTER

- timeline

- budget planner

- hebrew term glossary

Despite the many years that may stretch between now and the time your child turns thirteen, there are a few details of a bar mitzvah celebration that must be tended to early. Years in advance is not an exaggeration when it comes to beginning religious training. You should secure the date of the event, and start thinking about party location, entertainment, and other details at least two or three years out. Although it may seem overwhelming and premature at first, once you start thinking about and having fun with the plans, you can begin enjoying the event—long before it even happens. With the tricky questions of when and how to begin already answered, you will have an extraordinary sense of relief and the makings of a great celebration to plan later. Since the bar mitzvah is a two part event—the service and the party—you want to allot enough time to focus on each while thinking about how one will blend seamlessly into the other.

timeline

It's never too early to start **planning.** Locations, entertainment companies, photographers, and caterers can book up more than a year in advance. That's not to say if you've got less time, you'll have to settle for less – just **get started** now.

Two or three years ahead

- Hold date on synagogue calendar
- Alert family and friends (especially those who live out of town) of the bar or bat mitzvah date
- Draw up preliminary guest list
- Start working on budget

One to two years ahead

- Buy a planner to start tracking notes, information, ideas, and inspirations
- Firm up budget
- Visit and book reception locations
- Interview and hire event planner
- Interview and book photographer
- Interview and book videographer
- Interview and book entertainment company
- Interview and book band/deejay for reception
- Interview and book one-of-a-kind specialty entertainment
- Bar mitzvah child to select *mitzvah* project

Nine months to one year ahead

- Sign son or daughter up for bar or bat mitzvah classes at synagogue
- Interview and book caterer (if you will be hiring someone offsite)
- Interview and book event decorator or florist

Six to nine months ahead

- Mail "save-the-date" cards
- Visit possible local hotels and inns for out-of-town guests to stay and negotiate rate for block of rooms for these guests
- Begin shopping for outfits for children and adults
- Reserve any rental equipment, including tent, tables, chairs, and linen
- Book any transportation necessary, including for bar or bat mitzvah family as well as young guests and out-of-town company staying at hotels
- Order invitations and other necessary stationery, like "save-the-date" cards and thank-you notes
- Interview and book calligrapher

Four to six months ahead

- Plan and select favors
- Discuss any *oneg* Shabbat with synagogue caterer
- Meet with florist or event decorator to discuss bouquets, arrangements, etc.
- Arrange to hear deejay/emcee or musicians perform to help determine style and selection
- Try out and book makeup artist and hairstylist for for moms and daughters

Two to four months ahead

○ Meet with caterer to discuss menu anc schedule tasting
○ Schedule tasting for cake and place order
○ Meet with rabbi and/or cantor to discuss service
○ Have bar or bat mitzvah child begin wcrking on speech
○ Mail invitations

Four to six weeks ahead

○ Write programs; arrange for printing
○ Send congratulations announcement to synagogue newsletter
○ Provide deejay/emcee/band with "play" and "don't play" list
○ Send shot list to photographer and videographer
○ Start arranging seating plan

Two weeks ahead

○ Give caterer final guest count
○ Finalize seating plan; write or notify calligrapher for place cards
○ Schedule any necessary hair and beauty treatments

Cne week ahead

○ Check final details with all vendors
○ Go to bank to withdraw crisp bills for gratuities
○ Place gratuities in envelopes labeled appropriately

One day ahead

○ Moms and daughters go for manicures and pedicures
○ Relax

Joining a Synagogue

While most synagogues won't turn away anyone wanting to celebrate a bar mitzvah, most do require that families become members of the congregation. In fact, you will likely need to join several years before your child's thirteenth birthday so that he or she may attend religious school. But that's not the sole reason synagogues encourage you to join. "The most important thing that a family can do is to become a part of a religious community," says Rabbi Robert Levine of Congregation Rodeph Shalom in New York City. "Don't treat a bar mitzvah like one episode. Use it as a way to connect your family to a lifetime commitment." In areas with large Jewish populations there will typically be a few temples; areas with fewer Jews may only have one. If you are able to choose between synagogues, there are a variety of reasons why you may select one over the other. The level of observance is one: Reform, Reconstructionist, Conservative, or Orthodox. Others may include the rabbi, the school, the teachers, the number of families in the congregation, proximity to your home, days religious school is offered, and other factors. It pays to inquire about bar and bat mitzvah practices too. Likely you won't make your final decision based on the answers, but it is still good information to know. Do you get your choice of date? Will your child have to share the *bimah* with another child celebrating a bar mitzvah (called a b'nai mitzvah). Ask some questions about their approach to the ceremony. Will your child lead the service? Are you allowed to participate in the service? How is that affected if one of the parents is not Jewish? Do they encourage involvement from other congregants as well as from your special guests? The answers should provide a good sense of their view on children and families, and the philosophy of the rabbi and cantor. Anybody you interview should be happy to answer whatever queries they can and arrange for you to speak with someone else if necessary.

The Date

Choosing—or more likely, being assigned—a date for the service is a top priority and one synagogues usually see to about two to three years in advance. A guaranteed ceremony slot will ensure you have use of the sanctuary, and that the rabbi and cantor will be there; it also will determine a host of other details, such as when bar mitzvah training classes will begin and when a *mitzvah* project (a community service project usually required of anyone celebrating a bar mitzvah) needs to be completed. Knowing the date allows you to begin some of the legwork for the party, too, such as finding a place to hold it and hiring entertainment, which can already be booked well ahead of time (SEE CHAPTER FOUR, PARTY PLANS).

Since bat mitzvahs typically take place on a Saturday, most synagogues follow a structured system in order to accommodate all the congregants celebrating bat mitzvahs in a given year. When possible, synagogues will try to assign a date that corresponds with a child's birthday or is on a Shabbat day very close to it. Synagogues with a larger membership may book two events per day—one in the morning during the *shachareet* service and one in the late afternoon or evening for the *mincha* or *marev* service—or book even more than one bat mitzvah per service if necessary. The Torah is not usually taken out during *havdalah*—the service that closes Shabbat—or on Friday night, but some synagogues will make special accommodations. Consider yourself fortunate if the date you are given works for you, otherwise you may be in for some serious negotiating, especially in synagogues with a large b'nai mitzvah population; you may be put on a waiting list for a date other than the initial one offered. It's best to inquire about your synagogue's policy before accepting or declining any date.

If you know you will want a date that doesn't fall near your child's birthday—whether you need flexibility to accommodate out-of-town visitors, want a particular Torah portion that has significant meaning to your family, have your heart set on an outdoor celebration and your child's birthday is a winter one, or know there will be a conflict with a specific date—put in your preference early on. Of course, the date you ultimately settle on can be later than a thirteenth birthday (or for girls, earlier, since they are recognized as a bat mitzvah at the age of twelve, although most wait to celebrate the occasion until they are thirteen).

Holiday weekends are popular alternatives, especially ones that fall conveniently on the calendar. For example, if your child's birthday is in early February, you may plan for President's Day; for an early May birthday, you may want to wait for Memorial Day. These dates are often highly sought after since they allow family and friends to spend extra time together. It's important to note the downside

EARLY NEWS

A clever calendar save-the-date card provides information about your child's bar mitzvah celebration ahead of time.

September
2005

				1	2	3
4	5	6	7	8	9	(10)
11	12	13	14	15	16	17
18	19	20	21	22	23	24
25	26	27	28	29	30	

STEPHANIE GOLD
is being called to the Torah as a bat mitzvah
PLEASE SAVE THE DATE
Saturday, September 10, 2005

of special dates like these too. Travel for out-of-town guests is typically pricier and more hectic and reservations are harder to come by. Other holidays, like Mother's Day or New Year's, for instance, may seem particularly festive. Be aware, though, that costs for specialty items, like flowers and entertainment on these days will likely be more expensive as they are in greater demand. Still there are amazing possibilities for themes, decorations, and inspiration that a holiday can bring, not to mention the extra level of celebrating everyone feels inclined to do. Plus, the holiday will have all the more special meaning in the years that follow.

Next, with the date confirmed, go through all the proper motions at the synagogue. Find out if a deposit is required, and if there are any forms to fill out or any other formalities that need your attention. It is standard practice for synagogues to mail letters stating the date and time that has been reserved for a child's bar mitzvah; find out when and how you can expect notification. Make this the first piece of paper filed in your planner or organizer (SEE "ORGANIZATION AND INSPIRATION," PAGE 24).

The letter may or may not state if your son or daughter will share the *bimah* with another bar mitzvah child—don't hesitate to call the synagogue office to ask.

You may also choose to let family and good friends know the date. Two years before the date might be a bit earlier than necessary to make travel plans, but you never know. You may even be surprised: Some people may plan an extended vacation in the area and would appreciate knowing as early as possible so they can make their own arrangements. Either way, the date is exciting news to share.

COURSE LOAD
A Jewish education is
an integral part of the
experience. Children
will study history,
Hebrew, and the Torah.

Hebrew Classes and Religious Training

Classes and training sessions are required and necessary to help your child prepare for this experience. Curricula and hours of study required vary among synagogues. A typical schedule is as follows: religious school training begins as early as kindergarten, Hebrew school at the third grade level, and bar mitzvah training in the year or six months leading up to the event. Some synagogues even have programs for the whole family in the year or six months prior to the bar mitzvah that include a series of classes, activities, and projects that a family participates in together.

The hours required per week will also depend on the synagogue and whether it is Reform, Conservative, or Orthodox; expect the least amount for Reform synagogues and the most for Orthodox, with Conservative falling somewhere in between. If you and your child have to balance a slew of other activities and obligations, make a point to find out class times as far in advance as possible so you can work them into a busy schedule. You can expect most religious schools to teach the history of the Jewish people, a familiarity with the Torah, and different levels of Hebrew fluency for reading, writing, and conversation; they will also call for some mandatory attendance at weekday and Shabbat services so children understand the prayers and become comfortable leading the congregation. Some synagogues even require parents to be present at a certain number of services in the year before their child's bar mitzvah to supervise the group of kids there. Classes are typically age appropriate and parents should encourage their children with a new or renewed sense of interest so Hebrew school is not a chore but an enjoyable experience.

Who takes charge of bar mitzvah training is also dependent on the particular synagogue. Some cantors take on the task of teaching Torah and *haftarah* portions as well as assist with the *devar Torah* and speech writing. Other synagogues "foster a mentor program," says Cantor Judy Greenfeld of Temple Emanuel in Beverly Hills, CA, where a learned or scholarly member of the congregation reads over the portion with the child and then shows them how to look at commentary. Cantor Greenfeld, who was a mentor before her ordination, says she used to make the process more about discovery. "The job of the mentor or instructor," says Cantor Greenfeld, "is to find the part of the portion that the child can relate to. It is to uncover what treasure is there for him to receive, then to remind the child that will be his portion, every year at the same time for the rest of his life. And that makes it special." Many families and synagogues turn to tutors for bar mitzvah training as the number of children going through the process is

DANCE AND DINE
The traditional *horah* dance is typically in the mix of any party (far left). Tables placed around the dance floor is a popular setup for lunch or dinner (left).

so great, and many cantors and rabbis find they don't have the time to oversee the process as well as they would like. In theses cases, the cantor steps in only in the last few weeks, helping to polish the Torah portion and *haftarah*. Still, in smaller communities, both the cantor and rabbi may take a larger role in every aspect of the training.

The Party

For many people, the party after the ceremony is the all-out celebration—a time to show great pride in the bar or bat mitzvah, express joy, and to have a good time. The thorny part of planning the party—aside from making it a great event for both kids and adults—is to make it an amazing thirteen-year-old's bash while infusing it with all the meaning the day should bring. Yours can be a spectacular event, celebrating your child and all of his accomplishments, but it can be heartfelt too (SEE CHAPTER FOUR, PARTY PLANS).

As with the ceremony, you will be beholden to the date dictated by your synagogue if you choose to have the ceremony and the reception on the same day. The only restriction on time of day—morning, afternoon, or evening—is that the party should happen after the ceremony. Of course, more observant families will wait until after sundown or even Sunday to hold a party, considering certain Shabbat limitations. Many popular venues book a year or more ahead for weddings and other events so don't wait too long to begin your search. The location you ultimately choose will depend on many factors, including your budget, number of guests, and the season, to name a few (SEE CHAPTER FOUR, PARTY PLANS). Once you find a location, you can begin the fun part: planning the theme or party style with music, decorations, entertainment, and more. And during all the preparations, don't forget about a Friday night dinner and a Sunday brunch (if the celebration is on Saturday) for family and out-of-town guests. These events take much less planning, but still require some attention. They are wonderful additions to the festivities and can be quite meaningful in the end: Both give you a chance to spend some time with family and friends in a more intimate, less frenzied setting than the celebration.

Organization and Inspiration

Once you have taken these initial steps you will have some breathing room before the heavy-duty planning gets underway (SEE THE TIMELINE, PAGE 16). That doesn't mean you cannot or should not be thinking about the rest all the while. It helps to set up a system to keep your thoughts, ideas, and any information gathered in a convenient place from the start. Create a file on your computer, use a storebought planner, or make your own from

a three-ring binder with folders and dividers to track names and phone numbers and to keep notes and information from important meetings. You'll find the folders come in handy to store inspirational photos, compile magazine clippings, keep fabric swatches for table linens, dresses, and more. You will also want a place to keep business cards—every card from the temple administrator to the caterer and deejay should go in here so all the contact numbers are easy to find and accessible.

Create sections in your planner for any category you can think of, such as inspiration, budget, guest list, ceremony, *mitzvah* project, reception location, decorations/flowers, catering, photography and videography, music, entertainment, favors, candlelighting, speech, transportation, and hotel accommodations. You will also want a place to make lists, jot down notes, and record any thoughts that race through your mind.

Get or make a planner for your son or daughter too so he or she can take notes—especially after chatting with friends, attending other bar mitzvahs or parties, or even hearing a song from a new CD that is a must for the deejay to play. It's a great way to keep your child involved and let him or her know you welcome the input. And just remember, it's never too early to start thinking, planning, and getting organized—when you start really getting busy with all the details, you will be thrilled to have more than a head start.

Determining the Budget

Once your daydreaming has gotten the planning process in motion, you need to add a dose of reality by tackling the budget. This is probably as unfun as the planning will get, but absolutely necessary. Begin by making a preliminary guest list. The number of people you plan to invite will not only help allocate your funds—a budget for 100 guests can stretch a lot further than the same budget for 200, when you will pay for more meals, favors, centerpieces, and a larger cake—but will also determine the mood and style of your party. Keep this in mind when you set pen to paper. Do you want an intimate gathering of your closest friends and family or an enormous gala affair? Will you have a formal luncheon for family and your friends and a fun party for the kids at night? Is your extended family big or small? Does your child have lots of groups of friends he or she won't possibly want to leave out or is he or she more comfortable around a few close pals? For that matter, does your child do better in a small group rather than a crowd? If so, resist the urge to invite everyone in the neighborhood or your entire office staff. Also, if you all have your heart set on a specific location, whether a cozy historic hotel or the expansive grounds of a country club, the amount of people invited needs to fit comfortably, without feeling cramped or making the location

seem empty. But it's always more important to have the people you want there rather than booking the most fabulous space. That is the best reason to settle on your guest list first, then choose your space. (FOR MORE ON COMPILING A GUEST LIST, SEE CHAPTER FOUR, PARTY PLANS).

A realistic budget will also help you and your child firm up any visions and separate the must-have details from those you could live without. Only you and your family can determine just what resources will be used to pay for this event. Some folks put away money for years to pay for a celebration. Others plan to dip into their savings to come up with what they need. Still other people have saved for the occasion, but will use part of the money for a party and put the rest away as a gift to their child, in an account of his or her own for college, graduate school, a house, or just simply for spending.

And it is all a game of give and take. If there are areas where you or your child want to splurge, just be prepared to scale back elsewhere. Take decorations for instance. If you know you want to transform a plain, simple space into a magical place and it will take lots of material and manpower to do it, allocate more to the event decorating budget. Just be sure to decide where you can cut—maybe you offer fewer menu selections or instead of your child's first choice in favors, he or she opts for less expensive gifts.

There are quite a few ways to stretch your budget and make every dollar count. Brunches and luncheons are typically less costly than evening events; their time frame is shorter, the food served is lighter, and bar expenses can be minimal. For an evening event, serve just champagne and wine or a signature cocktail for grown-ups and soda for the kids. Choose either sparkling or flat water to trim costs—not both. Have the ceremonial cake be the dessert so there is no need for anything else. Buffets tend to be less expensive than formal seated meals, but depending upon the food served, this is not always the case (FOR MORE BUDGET TIPS, SEE CHAPTER FOUR, PARTY PLANS).

Since evening events are the most sought after, some locations offer discounted prices for morning and afternoon parties in order to book the space. The same holds true for events during January and February when other events, like weddings, are not as popular, so be sure to ask. If you will use flowers, choose ones that are in season or direct your florist to do so.

Consider storebought invitations run through your home computer or having invitations thermographed rather than engraved (SEE CHAPTER FIVE, INVITATIONS AND MORE). Do some things yourself or enlist the help of talented friends and family; for example, accept a friend's offer to act as photographer—but only if you have seen and really like his or her work. Your child may want to try her hand at calligraphy or come up with creative wrapping for favors; remember, though, you and your child will be busy with other details, so don't take on too much yourselves. Trim the guest list as much as you can and look for a location specializing in parties so you don't have to hire an outside caterer, rent items like tables and linens, or manage any other unforeseen extras. Look over contracts carefully, making sure to get prices in writing so you avoid any "fine print" charges after the fact. And as other details come up or suggestions are agreed upon, be flexible. You may want to trim the expense of one element of the party and add it to another to make a perfect party in the end.

The Role of Host

Assuming the proper role as host will go a long way toward assuring the success of the event. The first rule is to consider your guests' needs from the start. Mail "save-the-date" cards if you expect a number of out-of-town guests so that they may have as much notice as possible to plan their trip. These cards announce the date and time of the celebration, important for those who need to make plane and hotel reservations or take time off from work. If just a few guests will travel in, you can save on printing costs and create the cards on your home computer, handwrite notes, or make phone calls to share the details. It is thoughtful to provide the name of the nearest airport along with which airlines offer service there, as well as information on rail transportation if applicable. And since you cannot expect to meet every guest as they arrive in town—a lovely gesture but almost impossible logistically—provide the name and telephone number of local taxi or car services they may use.

If you live in an area with a large Jewish population or if your child shares his date with another child from the same school, there is a good chance your guest list may overlap with others. For this reason you may also choose to send "save-the-date" cards to local guests, so they can mark it on the calendar.

Visit area hotels, inns, or bed and breakfasts to find suitable lodging for out-of-town guests. Speak to the manager at each establishment to arrange any discount rates if possible. That information can be included with the "save-the-date" cards or as a separate insert in the invitation. When the date of the event nears, put together or organize gift baskets for guest rooms. Include any theme items, tasty snacks, an itinerary, local map, a list of local services and events, and favorite sites. Arrange for them to be placed in guests' rooms before they check in or given to the guests upon arrival.

If the party is more than a short distance from the synagogue, it is expected that you will arrange transportation, typically a van, bus, or ultra stretch limousine, for kids and chaperones to get to the party (parents are usually responsible for pick up). It is important to realize that it is then your responsibility to make sure all the

kids are accounted for. Make a bus list including every rider's name (compiled from the response cards and updated to the last minute) and give it to the chaperones, one of whom is hopefully familiar with the faces.

You need to see that invitations are sent out in a timely manner, at least eight to ten weeks in advance. It is advisable to send them out even earlier for a holiday weekend or if you know of other bar mitzvahs taking place the same day in your area. As host, it is up to you to ensure the caterer is aware of and able to accommodate any guests' dietary restrictions and that guests are seated appropriately, providing a good mix at each table and as close to or far away from the dance floor as you see fit (SEE CHAPTER FOUR, PARTY PLANS). You also want to see that rest rooms at the ceremony and reception site are properly outfitted and attended. Put together "convenience" baskets for the men's and ladies' rooms (SEE "FILLING REST ROOM BASKETS," APPENDIX, PAGE 139). At the ceremony it will be your job to make sure your child has everything he or she needs, but at the reception you need to see to your guests' comforts. You should mingle at the party and speak to each guest individually (you can talk to groups of kids since they are often not on their own), if only for a moment or two. It is your responsibility to check in with every professional at the party from the caterer to the photographer and entertainers to make sure all is running smoothly. You need to

ensure that the kids are being supervised and entertained. And at the end of the event, you want to see that favors are set up, gratuities handed out, and that everyone has a ride home. Your list of responsibilities may seem enormous, so if you are daunted by the size of the job, consider hiring a party planner (SEE "CONSIDERING AN EVENT PLANNER," PAGE 48) to assume some, if not all, of the burden. If you prefer to do it yourself, enlist the help of family or a few friends and assign some of these duties to them. If you don't, not only are some details bound to be missed, but, as you are mired in the little things, you may also miss the joy of the entire celebration.

GRAND ENTRANCE

Page 31: A synagogue's inner workings—clergy, congregation, and services—should be what draw you in. A beautiful exterior like this one of Central Synagogue in New York City makes arriving more fun.

budget
planner

ceremony

Synagogue fee

  Friday evening _____

  Saturday morning _____

Kippot _____

subtotal _____

reception

Event planner fee _____

Location fee _____

Caterer fee _____

  Food _____

  Bar _____

  Cake _____

  Professionals' meals _____

Rental fees _____

Bathroom basket _____

Transportation _____

Valet parking _____

Coat check _____

Gratuities

  Maitre d' _____

  Wait staff _____

  Rest room attendants _____

  Parking attendants _____

  Coat check attendants _____

subtotal _____

music/entertainment

Deejay/band fee _____

Emcee _____

Motivational dancers _____

Extra equipment _____

Side entertainment

  Arcades _____

  Crafts _____

  Games _____

  Photography _____

  Other _____

  Other _____

subtotal _____

decorations

Event decorator _____

Ceremony decoration

  Bimah _____

  Aisles/seats _____

Reception decoration

  Centerpieces _____

  Cake table _____

  Guest book table _____

  Favor table _____

  Buffet tables _____

  Rest rooms _____

  Kids' lounge _____

  Entry area _____

  Photography _____

  Lighting _____

  Fabric _____

  Upholstering _____

  Prop rentals _____

  Other _____

subtotal _____

other events

Friday night dinner for out-of-town guests _____

Friday night *oneg* Shabbat _____

Saturday morning *oneg* Shabbat _____

Morning-after brunch _____

subtotal _____

photography

Photographer fee _____

Additional prints _____

Additional services

  Slide show _____

  Montage _____

  Blowups _____

  Special effects _____

  Other _____

Videographer fee _____

Additional videos _____

Disposable cameras _____

subtotal _____

stationery/printed pieces

Design and printing costs

  Save-the-date cards _____

  Save-the-date envelopes _____

  Invitations/envelopes _____

  Reception cards _____

  Response cards _____

  Response envelopes _____

  Thank-you notes _____

  Thank-you envelopes _____

  Ceremony programs _____

  Menu _____

  Other _____

Postage

  Invitation envelopes _____

  Response card envelopes _____

  Thank-you envelopes _____

Calligraphy

  Invitation envelopes _____

  Escort/place cards _____

  Table numbers _____

  Party favor labels _____

Other stationery items

  Guest sign-in book _____

  Custom design work _____

  Other _____

subtotal _____

miscellaneous

Attire _____

Favors _____

Rest room baskets _____

Hotel guest baskets _____

Other _____

subtotal _____

Ceremony _____

Reception _____

Music/Entertainment _____

Decorations _____

Other Events _____

Photography _____

Stationery/Printed pieces _____

Miscellaneous _____

TOTAL _____

hebrew terms

aliyah

(plural is *aliyot*) literally means going up, as in going up to the *bimah*. The bar mitzvah child or others are called upon to say a prayer over the Torah or to read from the Torah.

bimah

is the pulpit from which the service is conducted and where the Torah is read, and the ark is positioned.

devar (or d'var) Torah

is an explanation of the Torah portion. This may be delivered by the b'nai mitzvah, the rabbi, or another learned member of the congregation.

haftarah

are writings and commentary by prophets that are meant to be synchronized with each Torah portion. They are presented after the final Torah portion is read. The b'nai mitzvah typically says the prayer before the *haftarah* portion, chants the *haftarah*, and recites the final prayer after.

havdalah

marks the end of Shabbat. The service itself is relatively short but quite beautiful and powerful. The Torah is not typically read during *havdalah*, although exceptions can be made.

mincha and marev (or ma'ariv)

are the afternoon and evening services. On Shabbat, the Torah is taken out during these services but only three portions are read.

minyan

is a group of ten Jewish adults required for communal prayer (men only in Orthodox service).

oneg Shabbat

is a selection of desserts and drinks following the service on Friday evening and Saturday mornings. The *kiddush* and *hamotzi* blessings are both said for the *oneg*, which is usually sponsored by the bar mitzvah family. Sometimes the words *kiddush* and *oneg* are used interchangeably.

parasha

are the Torah portions read each week. The Torah is divided into fifty-four *parasha*.

shachareet

is the morning service. On Shabbat, this service is the longest, with seven Torah portions, and it is the most popular time for bar mitzvahs.

tallis

(plural is *tallisim*) is the prayer shawl worn on Shabbat by men over the age of thirteen (strictly observant men wear a smaller *tallis* under their clothes every day; in many modern congregations, women also wear *tallisim*). While the fabric of the *tallis* has no real significance, the fringes dangling from each of the four corners do; the Torah requires the wearing of fringes to symbolize the Commandments.

tzedakah

means charity or giving. It is considered a *mitzvah* or good deed.

Torah

is the holy scripture given to the Jewish people by God. It contains commandments and laws and the history of the Jewish people. The Torah is divided into five books—Genesis, Exodus, Leviticus, Numbers, and Deuteronomy—which are read on an annual cycle.

2

CEREMONY SPEAK

IN THIS CHAPTER

- Torah primer

- choosing a service

- involving family and friends

Who said a thirteen-year-old is an adult? Well, in the Jewish religion, it seems as though Talmudic scholars did. These men interpreted the Torah and, perhaps noting that both Abraham and Jacob took firm ideologic stands at age thirteen, deemed this the age when a boy would become a bar mitzvah and automatically assume the grown-up responsibilities of the commandments, recite blessings over the Torah, count in a *minyan*, and more. Today the term bar mitzvah refers to the boy and to the ceremony he participates in to mark the occasion. The ceremony is steeped in tradition, yet it is a relatively modern rite in Jewish history. It wasn't until sometime between the fourteenth and sixteenth centuries, and only in a few European countries with religious freedom, that the bar mitzvah ceremony began. The custom of the bat mitzvah is even newer. Some believe its origins came from Rabbi Mordecai Kaplan, a forward-thinking New York City rabbi, who in 1922 presided over the bat mitzvah of his daughter, Judith. Others believe the first bat mitzvah might have taken place a century before in Europe. Whatever the religious roots, the bar and bat mitzvah are popular and respected customs today and ones that require plenty of dedication and preparation from you and your child to ensure that either event will be as special and meaningful as it should be.

Understanding the Torah

Even if you spent your childhood in religious school, went to Jewish summer camp, and celebrated your own bar mitzvah, some details of Jewish history can fade. Since reading from the Torah has become the cornerstone of modern bar mitzvahs, here is a quick refresher on its origins and makeup. The Torah, which was given to the Jewish people by God and contains the laws, commandments, and history of our people, are sacred scrolls whose stories are read on an annual cycle. The Torah has fifty-four portions, or *parasha*, that are read, throughout the year, beginning on the fall holiday of *Simchat Torah* (three weeks following *Rosh Hashanah*) with the book of Genesis. Each week following, one (or two on a couple of weeks) *parasha*, divided into seven sections (or *aliyot*), is read, in order, from the other four books (Exodus, Leviticus, Numbers, Deuteronomy), with the entire cycle completing on the following *Simchat Torah*. What is truly amazing is that any child becoming a bar mitzvah on a particular day will be chanting or reading the same laws, scripture, history, and stories as any other child becoming a bar mitzvah on the same day, anywhere in the world—an emotionally charged idea that ties your child to the past and the present all at the same time.

If your child is assigned a bar mitzvah date—and thereby a portion—close to his birthday, the following explanation from Rabbi Robert Tobin of The Conservative Synagogue in Westport, CT will give you a general notion of what your child will be studying and reading about: The first book of the Torah, Genesis, is read during the fall to early winter months. It includes stories about the world's creation and the early legends of Abraham and Sarah, Isaac and Rebecca, and Jacob, Rachel, and Leah. The second book, Exodus, is read between midwinter and early spring. The portions in Exodus discuss the exodus of the Jewish people from Egypt, their journey to Mount Sinai, receiving the Ten Commandments, and building their sanctuary in the wilderness. The book of Leviticus, read in springtime, covers laws of sacrifices and priestly obligations, social legislation, and guidelines for holiness. The stories in the book of Numbers, which are read from late spring through early summer, chronicle the Jewish people through the next thirty-eight years in the desert. Finally, in the summer to early fall, the last portions of the Torah are read in Deuteronomy. These are Moses' swan song, a retelling of the story of Israel and a strong as well as poetic reminder of the Jewish people's obligations on the eve of entering the Land of Israel.

אֱלֹהִים בַּיָּם וַיֹּאמֶר לֵי אֶ

בְּתוֹךְ הַיָּם יַבָּשָׁה כָהֶם וַיֻּבֶּה בַּיָּם

בַּיָּבָּשָׁה. בְּתוֹךְ הַיָּם אֶת יִשְׂרָאֵל מִיַּד מִצְרַיִם

יָהִיד בַּיּוֹם הַהוּא אֶת יִשְׂרָאֵל אֶת הַיָּד

מִתְעַל שְׂפַת הַיָּם וַיִּירְאוּ וַיַּאֲמִינוּ

בְּמִצְרַיִם וַיִּירְאוּ הָעָם אֶת יְהוָה וַיַּאֲמִינוּ

אָז יָשִׁיר מֹשֶׁה וּבְנֵי יִשְׂרָאֵל אֶת דְּ

לֵאמֹר אֲשִׁירָה לַ

יִרְכְּבוּ רְכֻדְ. בַּיָּם

לִישׁוּעָה

אָבֵל וְאַ

MAKING SHABBAT

Most ceremonies take place on the Sabbath, when special prayers are said over the candles, wine, and *challah*.

Deciding the Time and Type of Service

Planning the ceremony is really less about planning than preparing. After all, the service itself—or, rather, several services—are already in place. In the most basic ceremony, the bar mitzvah is called to the *bimah* to recite a blessing over the Torah (or is given an *aliyah*). So, really, a bat mitzvah can take place on any day the Torah is read: For most Conservative and Orthodox synagogues this is Saturday mornings and afternoons, and Mondays and Thursdays. Most reform synagogues only have a Saturday Torah reading when there is a bat mitzvah taking place. The Torah is also read on *rosh chodesh* (the first of the month on the Jewish calendar) and on holidays, although it is less common for a bat mitzvah to take place then or on a Friday night Shabbat service.

Most ceremonies take place on Saturday (Orthodox girls may have a comparable service on Sunday since it is not permitted for them to read from the Torah) and many synagogues will offer a choice of services: There are a few throughout the day. If your synagogue does not and you have a preference, why not ask if they will accommodate your request? The time of day will depend on the length of service you favor, the level of preparation your child is willing to devote, travel concerns for guests, and even the type of reception you envision and the budget for that party.

The Morning Service

The *shachareet*, or Shabbat morning service, is standard and preferred by many for a number of reasons. For starters, it is grand in substance and tradition. "The Torah reading is longer than in the afternoon, which allows for more people from the family and congregation to participate in this core element of the service," says Rabbi Tobin. There are seven *aliyot* in the morning. If your child will recite the entire day's portion, there are seven portions and the *haftarah* (writings from prophets to go along with each weekly Torah portion) to learn. He may deliver a *devar Torah*, which is an explanation of the weekly Torah portion as well. So you will want to factor in his motivation, dedication, and time allowance before committing to such a considerable, yet rewarding, undertaking. When more than one child shares the *bimah* for the service, *aliyot*, readings, and even the *haftarah* are split equally among them.

Every service is open to the community and Saturday morning services are typically well attended. Count on being host for the *oneg* Shabbat, which is a light spread of finger foods and beverages—as well as *challah* and wine for the *hamotzi* and *kiddush*—set out for the congregation after the service. Most morning services begin around nine thirty or ten o'clock and conclude around noon, which is the perfect time to plan a luncheon or afternoon reception. This flow from the ceremony to the

party keeps everyone's energy and excitement high. Venues, catering, and entertainment costs are typically lower for daytime events. If you will have an evening party, the morning service allows a sufficient break in the day with plenty of time to recharge, visit with out-of-town guests, and to change outfits.

For some, the morning service is not ideal in combination with an evening party, especially if they will have guests who live close enough to drive for the day, but not so close that they can easily run home in between events. In this case, the bar mitzvah family will open their home to guests for the break in festivities. This is a wonderful gesture indeed, although one with added planning details and one that leaves little time to refresh for the evening ahead. The break in events is also a natural break in the feel and mood of the festivities, and for some, one they may not want to make.

The Afternoon to Evening Services

The afternoon into evening services, or *mincha* and *marev*, are shorter than those in the morning and a bit more subdued. There are only three *aliyot* and no *haftarah*, which is ideal for kids with an otherwise busy schedule and limited time to commit or who feel more comfortable focusing on a smaller task. This also means there are only three blessings over the Torah to offer family and close friends. Still, there are a number of ark openings and other honored roles to offer such as holding, dressing, and carrying the Torah. The timing, anywhere from late afternoon to early evening in the winter and early evening to mid-evening in the summer, is a natural segue to an evening reception. And since the majority of congregants who attend Shabbat services do so in the morning, your crowd will mostly be limited to invited guests. It is not likely you will even have to sponsor an *oneg* Shabbat following an afternoon or evening service—one way to save in planning and expense.

Havdalah, the service that brings Shabbat to a close is a beautiful, poignant, and relatively short service and one that usually does not include a Torah reading. Certain synagogues will make exceptions, but many people who want this ceremony for its spirit as well as its convenient time slot will hold it elsewhere so as not to be bound by the rules.

Taking Part in the Service

In any service, the child may lead the congregants in prayer, have an *aliyah*, recite the weekly Torah portions, chant the *haftarah* (only during *shachareet* services), and deliver the *devar Torah*. Some synagogues encourage bat mitzvahs to partake in all of these elements, others suggest concentrating on just a few, and still others leave the decision of how much or how little to do to the child and parents.

Once the type of service is determined, then the education, exploration, learning, and preparation begins. Training classes are both group and individual and start about six months to a year before the date of the ceremony. Your child can expect to learn the service, his or her Torah portion, and the *haftarah* (SEE "HEBREW CLASSES AND RELIGIOUS TRAINING," PAGE 23).

Involving Family and Friends

Your child is not the only who can prepare for the ceremony. You can too. One of the best ways to make the service most meaningful is for you and other family members to participate as well. Discuss with your rabbi how you and your family can get more involved. Certainly you can have an *aliyah* or other honor. Also ask about reciting a parents' prayer—there are many readings and psalms that are perfectly appropriate for occasions such as this. If you would rather write your own, ask for guidelines from your rabbi. You might even ask about the week's Torah portion to draw on the names, characteristics, and histories of any people discussed in it. Doing so is a helpful starting point for a speech and a good way to tie thoughts and feelings to the traditions of the day. It's best to keep your speech short, especially if your son or daughter is sharing the *bimah* with another child. Not only will you be emotional, but you will also have plenty of time at the party later to share your feelings about how special your child is and how much the day means to you.

According to Rabbi Tobin, "other minor honors are also allocated during each service, such as opening or closing the ark, raising and dressing the Torah scroll, holding the scroll while the *haftarah* is read, or reading a prayer in English or Hebrew." Find out from your rabbi who is eligible for what. For instance, are there some things only men can do or does a person have to be bar mitzvah age? Can couples come up together and can those who are not Jewish participate? Find out if there is particular dress required for anyone who will stand on the *bimah*. For *aliyot*, the rabbi will need all the names—Hebrew and English—of the participants ahead of time. Let those people who you will ask to be involved know ahead of time. This way they will be honored before the event and be prepared. It is also thoughtful to send a copy of a particular prayer to be read or the blessing over the Torah to those with an *aliyah* so they can practice if need be.

There are still other ways to bring significance to the occasion. Set out a special goblet for the *kiddush*, perhaps the one you drank from at your wedding, one that has been used by your family for other special events, or one you purchase just for the occasion and hope will be used for generations. Make a program for congregants to follow: List the order of the service and the

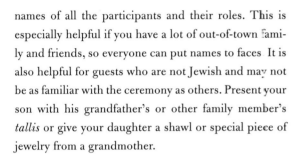

CUP COLLECTION

The *kiddush* cup holds the ceremonial wine. Give a special cup as a gift to the bar mitzvah child or use a family heirloom that has been passed down for generations.

names of all the participants and their roles. This is especially helpful if you have a lot of out-of-town family and friends, so everyone can put names to faces. It is also helpful for guests who are not Jewish and may not be as familiar with the ceremony as others. Present your son with his grandfather's or other family member's *tallis* or give your daughter a shawl or special piece of jewelry from a grandmother.

Arranging Off-Site Ceremonies

The synagogue is the typical place, but not the only one in which to hold the service. Reasons to look for alternative sites are many. One is that a family wants to personalize the service but the clergy at their synagogue are not entirely receptive to the idea. "People need to honor their children as individuals," says Cantor Judy Greenfeld of Temple Emanuel in Beverly Hills, CA. "Clergy need to do creative services; not outrageous ones but ones that are done with integrity. It is important for the bar mitzvah child to see that his parents and the community are honoring who he is." Other reasons include that the family feels this is too special an occasion to share the spotlight with another bar mitzvah, or that there is a place that holds significant meaning for the child or the family. "Since the bar mitzvah ceremony itself is a recent creation, there is no formal requirement regarding how it should be celebrated," says Rabbi

Tobin, although he notes, "it is generally considered most fitting to mark the child's new status as an adult within his or her community by taking a leadership role in that community's synagogue." Still, he adds, "it is possible for families to design their own locations—a home, the beach, Israel—and hold their own services."

With this decision come many logistical details and religious elements that otherwise would be taken care of by synagogue staff, including bar mitzvah training, the presence of clergy, a Torah scroll, and more. Contact local Judaic study centers and universities for bar mitzvah tutors; rabbinic and cantoral interns can tutor your child and lead the service too. Talk to family friends or other congregants who are well-schooled in Judaic studies and ask for their assistance. You may want your child to go through training at the synagogue. And ask if it is possible for you to borrow a Torah for the service. If you are planning your service at the same place as your reception, make sure that the look and feel is appropriate. Find out if the site coordinator has any experience with bar mitzvah ceremonies and is willing to accommodate your needs. If you are thinking about a public space, like a park or beach, inquire about permits and whether there is any element of privacy or if uninvited guests will be allowed to wander in. If you will have the ceremony at home, think practically: you'll need tents to protect against rain or strong sun; hard,

GIFT PACKAGES
Presents come in all
shapes and sizes:
Some people bring an
item, others give
money toward a child's
savings, while still oth-
ers make a donation in
honor of the
bat mitzvah child.

even ground on which to set up chairs; and a safe place for the ark and Torah. Destination ceremonies are even a bit more complicated, since you have to transport your immediate family and assist in helping arrange your guests' transportation too. You also need to arrange all the logistical and religious details long distance, which can be trying. Again, this is a project you can take on alone or with an event planner who undoubtedly is able to solve a multitude of problems with a skilled hand.

Choosing a *Mitzvah* Project

The *mitzvah* project is required of a bat mitzvah child at many synagogues. It typically needs to be planned and completed before the bat mitzvah date. The purpose of the project is to teach children responsibility to community and a hands-on understanding of *tzedakah*, or charity. Work with your child to choose a *mitzvah* project. Ideally it is something to help your local community, Israel, even the environment, and should serve as a reminder that she should being taking on mature responsibilities in the world around her. Educators at your synagogue should also help generate ideas and sources that will help with your child's undertaking and completion of this project. Urge her to choose something you can become involved with too. And kids don't have to stop with one project (although don't let them take on too much either).

A group effort is another way to go. At Congregation Rodeph Shalom in New York City, the seventh grade students do not give gifts to each other for their bar and bat mitzvahs. In lieu of presents, they pool whatever money would have been spent and create a *tzedakah* collective. Representatives of chosen charitable organizations then come to the school to give presentations, children learn about the charities, then select one or more to which they will disperse thousands of dollars. It is a wonderful lesson in the true sense of *tzedakah*.

A Parent's Presence

Most important, a bar mitzvah is a family event as well as a community one. Make sure you stay involved so that the experience does not just become about your child learning the prayers and the Torah and with your role being shuttling him back and forth to lessons. If you feel a part of the process, you will also grow to have an understanding from a parent's perspective, with a wonderful newfound respect for your son as he grows, learns, and reaches this significant milestone. So share it together: Attend Shabbat services as a family; listen to your child practice his Torah or *haftarah* portion and learn the story behind it so you can discuss it with your child. And always, even when practice becomes a bit of a chore for both of you, let your child know just how proud you are.

3

MEET THE PROFESSIONALS

IN THIS CHAPTER

- finding the right people

- understanding contracts

- tipping guide

They will guide you, assist you, plan for you, prepare for you, sing for you, play for you, dress you, decorate for you, coordinate for you, entertain for you, capture memories for you, and more. Just who are they and where do they come from? They are the skilled professionals whose business it is to help make your party fabulous and whom you will turn to time and again for expertise, ideas, and advice. They are everywhere; you just need to find the ones best suited to you. The right professional will not only have strong references, offer inspiration, and be reliable, but he or she will also have a true understanding of yours and your child's visions, your budget, your needs, and your desires. And the results will be a wonderful reflection of all of that.

WAIT STAFF
WARDROBE

Waiters may wear cutfits
to reflect the party's
theme or color scheme.
If not, neutrals are
a must to blend into
the background.

Getting Recommendations

One of the best ways to find professionals is speak with family and friends. Find out if they can introduce you to anyone who they have worked with personally or if they can ask other family or friends for names. A personal recommendation from someone you trust is a strong starting point.

Stay focused when you attend parties now, from intimate gatherings to gala affairs. Take note if anything, such as flowers, music, or food, strikes your fancy. Speak to anyone responsible for making a good impression on you. Once you begin booking professionals, you can tap them for other resources —they likely know people in other fields. You can also try calling or searching online for organizations that can give you a list of event services in your area.

Meeting Professionals

Schedule meetings with any potential specialist, even those who come highly recommended or whose work you have seen before. You want to ensure he understands your needs and desires and that you are comfortable working with this person. Any professional should be happy to answer questions, offer ideas and inspiration, and be eager to show you samples of his work. Get at least three references from any person you are considering hiring; even if you have the most amazing meet-

ing, no one will be insulted if you ask. In fact, it is expected. Anyone who refuses or cannot produce any references is someone to be wary of.

It is also wise to meet with at least two or more professionals in a field. Even if you hit it off well with your first interview, keeping other scheduled appointments won't be a waste of your time. You might gather some useful information, reaffirm your desire to hire the other guy, or even end up meeting someone you like better. On the other hand, do not schedule a slew of meetings just because you think there might be someone you are missing out on. Sitting down with too many folks will be overwhelming not to mention time-consuming. It is best to narrow your search to three or four candidates. Any more than that and you will start to forget who said what even if you did take good notes.

That said, take along a notebook or pad to write down key points of your meetings so you will be able to link a brilliant idea or one you didn't like with the right person. You also want to come prepared with questions to ask. Jot them down in the same notebook for easy reference and keep all your notes in one place. That way you can flip between interviews to compare answers and revisit conversations. And once you make a decision, don't hesitate to hire that person. Chances are, if you like someone enough to want to work with them, other people will too. Don't get caught waiting too long or you will find the person you really want is no longer available.

Understanding Contracts

Once you have booked a professional, you will likely be asked to sign a contract for services rendered and to pay a deposit. Before you sign any contract, read it carefully, making sure you understand every phrase and line. If necessary, ask a lawyer to review it for you. While each contract will be specific to the particular service mentioned, each will also cite certain fundamentals. These include the date and day of the week of the event, location with the address, times the vendor or professional should arrive and can expect to stay until, the date and day of the week any delivery or pickup is to be made if necessary, explanation of service, contact information for the day of the party, liability insurance, and attire of professionals. Every contract should also stipulate the fee, deposit paid, and balance due with date. Overtime charges, taxes, and required gratuities should also be stated. If there are any outstanding prices due to uncertainty about guest list size, market prices, and the like, there should be a clause outlining the details noting a general amount due and a ceiling that the cost will not exceed.

No details should ever be open-ended, whether monetary concerns, the color of decorations, or music played. It all needs to be in writing. Any changes made along the way, by you or the professional, should be written down too. Even if you have a wonderful and friendly relationship, remember this process is still business and it is best to treat it as such. With every point documented, there is nothing left to question. In the following chapters, note contract points specific to stationers, event decorators, musicians, entertainers, photographers, and videographers. Be sure to get every point clarified; you should be completely comfortable with what you are signing. You and the vendor should sign both copies of the contract—one is for the vendor to keep and one is for you.

Considering an Event Planner

One professional in particular does not fall into any particular category, but straddles them all: the party planner or consultant. Hiring one might seem like an indulgence at first, but soon you will find working with a planner can save you time, effort, even money. Most planners are flexible, offering different services to meet your needs. You can hire a planner to help with every aspect of the party or to just be on call to help with specific tasks. They can help you find a location, decide on a style, even set a budget. And since planners are always working with other professionals, they can be not only a very good resource but can also negotiate discounted fees for passing on so many clients. If you will play a big role in planning your event, but feel you need an extra hand making sure everything runs smoothly on the day, you can hire a planner to oversee the actual event so you

tipping guide

You have worked very closely with your bar mitzvah event team—to great success—and a gratuity will surely be an appreciated gesture. Sometimes the gratuity is left to your discretion; at other times it is stipulated as a service charge in a contract. In that case, you can give more if you feel the service is extraordinary, but any extra is certainly not necessary (keep in mind that no tip is given to business owners such as florists and photographers). Plan gratuities ahead of time to avoid last-minute frenzy: Go to the bank, ask for crisp bills, and place them in pre-addressed envelopes.

PROFESSIONAL	GRATUITY
Party Planner	gift

A token such as a gift certificate, as well as a stellar recommendation, make the best tip for someone who has played such a big part in making the bar mitzvah celebration spectacular.

Rabbi/Cantor (Synagogue)	donation

It is not proper to tip clergy. A donation to the synagogue is perfectly appropriate and appreciated.

Caterer, Maître d', Wait Staff	15 to 20 percent

This is one contract that may stipulate a gratuity. If yours does, know that senior level staff receives a higher percentage than others. If you are unsure, ask the caterer what is customary.

Bartenders	10 to 15 percent

Sometimes a bartender's tip will be stated in the catering contract. If not, use this suggested percentage of the liquor charge.

Musicians, Deejay, and other Entertainers	$20 to $50 each

Tipping varies among entertainers. The amount you give will depend on each person's role.

Restroom and Coatroom Attendants	$1 to $2 per guest

These tips will come from you, not your guests. Make it clear to the caterer or party planner that no tips from guests should be accepted or solicited.

Deliverymen	$5 to $10 each

These service people will arrive well before you. Make sure someone, like your caterer or party planner, is on hand to distribute envelopes.

Parking Valets	$1 to $2 per car

These tips will come from you, not your guests. Make it clear to the valet manager that no tips from guests should be accepted or solicited.

MAKING FLOWERS

A florist may arrange
the flowers at his or her
studio ahead of time,
then make final touches
at the party site.

don't have to. You can also count on planners to point out details you had not considered or help you be in two places at once.

Again, find a planner by speaking with friends or family who have worked with one before, or ask other professionals whom they recommend. Once you collect names, you will want to interview potential planners to determine if their style is consistent with yours, if they understand what you want and need, if they will work within your budget, and if you will be comfortable working with them. Ask how many other projects they will take on during the time you will be working with them and if they will have sufficient time to spend on your event. Ask what the fee is and how it is charged. Some planners charge by the hour or by the service they provide, and others charge a percentage of the total cost of the event. Be sure to get in writing what the total cost will be, and if it is a percentage of the budget, make sure the contract specifies the percentage and a ceiling on the total fee. You will also want the contract to stipulate just what the planner is responsible for, whether it is helping you find other professionals, planning your entire event, or scouting locations.

Time and Day

Most professionals charge a higher fee for Saturday night services than for any other time during the week. Saturday evening is the most sought after time slot for special occasion celebrations and therefore professionals charge a premium. Holding a luncheon on Saturday or a Sunday brunch will keep catering costs down because these meals are typically less expensive than a dinner would be. The music will likely be more subdued at a function like this and therefore less elaborate and less expensive too. Location fees are often discounted for Sunday or midweek parties, and professionals such as photographers, entertainment vendors, and the like don't book up as quickly for these dates— they have even been known to decrease their fees in order to book a gig.

THROUGH THE LENS

Any photographer
should work the room
for candids and set up
a location for formal
shots too.

4

PARTY PLANS

IN THIS CHAPTER

- party style

- choosing a location

- menu ideas

Once the service has been scheduled, honors and *aliyot* assigned, and religious preparation undertaken, most of your attention will focus on the celebration to follow. Just what kind of celebration depends on many factors, including you and your child, your budget, the time of day, the season, the guest list, the level of creativity, and your desire to acknowledge the reason for the party in the first place. Some critics argue that a party after the service doesn't reflect the reason for the celebration or honor the seriousness and sanctity of the occasion. But no one needs to apologize for throwing a party. It is a wonderful way to share your joy with friends and family and for your bar mitzvah child to celebrate and be celebrated for a job well done. And even the most spectacular event can be heartfelt too. There are innumerable ways to infuse your party—whether a subtle affair or a blowout bash—with meaningful and appropriate details. Then there are those points that are all about style, ideas, and fun. First start with the basics outlined in the following pages, then focus on the details. Have a good time with them, be creative and resourceful, keep them simple, or make them over the top. Just remember that these details shape the day, transforming this special occasion into a most magical and memorable experience.

Thinking First

As discussed before, planning an event of this magnitude, and one that caters to pre-teens and grown-ups alike, can be as overwhelming as it is exciting. So before you get carried away with—or by—it all, take time to gather your thoughts. Do a little daydreaming, consider what you want, and discuss your child's desires. Draw on other parties or gatherings you've been to, both those celebrating a bar mitzvah and those observing other events, to think about what you like and don't like. Look for inspiration anywhere and everywhere; you'd be surprised where the best ideas come from. Friends and family are a good place to start. Many have planned their own events and have been guests at countless others. They might remember important details, recall aspects that were less successful, and may even have names of professionals whom they highly recommend. Talk to as many people as you can and ask to look through their event photo albums to spark even more ideas.

The media is also a useful source; teen and entertainment magazines are excellent for hot trends and theme ideas, home magazines are perfect for decorating and color scheme thoughts, bridal magazines can generate favor and catering inspiration, and fashion magazines are super for, well, fashion. Start watching television shows and movies in a whole new way; Hollywood has a knack for putting on the most amazing productions (albeit with out-of-this-world budgets) and you could undoubtedly pick up an idea or two from there as well. Go to the bookstore or library to peruse party planning books for ideas.

Then, of course, there is your child. Use his activities and interests to generate some more ideas for themes, colors, flowers, even the song list to give the deejay. Don't overlook a thing. Sometimes the littlest details turn into the most successful ideas. A girl, for instance, who has her walls at home plastered with snapshots of friends may love to have an old-fashioned photo booth at her bat mitzvah. These booths become activites and are wonderful for capturing spontaneous moments and special memories that even the best photographer could not hope to record. Or if your son has a favorite sports team—whether it's a professional basketball team or his own school's baseball team—use their uniform's colors for chair covers, table linens, centerpieces, and more.

Nothing you imagine needs to be concrete at this point; just think of it all as a good starting point. Certain ideas can even begin a domino effect, helping with other decisions down the line. And once you have a vision, you can start moving forward with the plans. That doesn't mean you need to book all your professionals in one week; it does mean that you can take some of the pressure off. In fact, while there are certain plans that need to be reserved early on, some others are best left until later. The following pages explain what to tackle right away and what can wait.

The Basics

Style

First off, you need to narrow down some fundamentals, such as the style of event and whether you want it to be formal or informal. Only then will you be able to make other key decisions like the time of day, location, attire, and menu. Evening parties are typically more formal than morning and afternoon events. That's not to say a luncheon has to be casual, it's just not appropriate to call for black tie and long gowns at two o'clock in the afternoon. There's no rule about formal versus informal in terms of location; an outdoor garden party can be equally as grand or casual as a bash at the swankiest country club. But common sense should prevail. If you will have a surfing theme in a hotel ballroom at night, formal is fine. It won't work if you will have a true surf scene on the beach all afternoon and a luau complete with tiki torches to follow.

Spirit

The style of the event will also affect the mood it evokes—an important point when planning a party for kids and adults. Decide what type of reception works best for your crowd. It may be lunch or dinner following the ceremony or even a brunch the next day. Some families do a cocktail party of sorts with passed hors d'oeuvres and drinks including a selection of fun non-alcoholic beverages for the kids. For a meal, you need to think whether you would prefer a seated meal that is served by wait staff or a buffet; if you will have assigned tables with place cards or just a smattering of chairs and tables so guests find seats with whomever they choose; or a separate kids' lounge or club area.

The final decision may come down to your budget. Dinner is typically the priciest meal since there are more courses and each is more elaborate than the next. You can also bet on a bigger bar bill for the adults as they will likely drink more in the evening than they would in the morning or afternoon. It's also popular to create a selection of non-alcoholic drinks for the kids for the nighttime celebrations. Lunch receptions can be equally tasteful, even fancy, but the food is generally lighter than it would be at dinner and is less costly. The same is true for brunches, even though you can offer some of the most sophisticated menus for either brunch or lunch that can cost as much as any dinner would. Also keep in mind the service style. Seated meals are more formal than buffets (SEE "WORKING WITH THE CATERER," PAGE 59) and can set the mood and tone for your event as much as the time of day or any menu could.

Guest List

The number of guests in attendance will certainly affect the feel of the event. A small, intimate gathering will be much different from a large crowd, whether they are

refined or rambunctious. Figure a rough estimate of guests to know the size group you need to accommodate. The guest list will determine the location space and your budget too. Caterers charge per person; centerpieces need to be set at every table and the more people, the more tables; each guest gets a favor, and so on. Begin with two lists, one for your guests and one for your child's. You can set a general limit from the start so she doesn't go overboard. Or review the initial result then pare down if necessary. You may find you can easily whittle down the original number or that there is no room at all to maneuver. The final list will be a combination of your list and your child's. And there really is no right number. Every family is different. Some might want to include only local relatives while others wouldn't think of not inviting far-flung family and friends. Many people consider certain members of their congregation extended family and include them as well. It is also proper to invite your rabbi and cantor and their respective spouses too.

Start your list with immediate family, then add on extended family, friends, and any business associates you feel compelled to invite. If the list starts spiraling out of control, one way to limit invitees is to only include people whom your child knows. Etiquette calls for asking significant others of your friends or relatives to attend when they are married, engaged, or living together. You may want to invite both members of couples in long-term relationships. Again, to keep size and costs down there is no need to invite single friends or family with a date, although if you can, it is always a thoughtful gesture.

Choosing a Location

Perhaps most important, think about where you would like it all to happen. The location you choose, whether the synagogue reception hall or your own backyard, is the backdrop for it all and needs to be worthy of a celebration as fabulous as this. Start scouting early. The places you are looking at are likely being considered by others planning bar mitzvahs, weddings, and other events, and many book up well in advance, maybe a year or more. In general, there are two types of locations: those that cater to large events and those that don't. You can have a fantastic celebration at either, but the latter will likely require more planning.

Let's talk first about those spots that are set up to hold special events like bar mitzvahs, such as hotels, restaurants, catering halls, country clubs, even your synagogue. Likely they have an in-house caterer, or at least kitchen facilities and caterers they work with regularly. They may even have an inventory of (or access to) tables, linens, china, silver, glassware, and more. There is ample and easy parking, perhaps even valet service. In colder months, they have a coat check room and well-kempt restrooms. Most venues like this hold multiple events every weekend and more during the week and are expert in helping you plan the party and making it run smoothly. You can have virtually no responsibility for minutiae if you choose. Some places will charge a location fee and others will roll it into the overall price. Expect the price you are quoted to be based on a per person calculation and to include basic choices for everything from the menu to the table settings to the dance floor. Many sites offer a degree of variety and may allow you to upgrade, for a fee, certain elements like menu selections, decorative chairs, linens, china, or the dance floor. If you bring in your own accessories and pieces you've rented elsewhere, be sure you are allowed to do so and find out if you will be charged an additional usage fee by the site.

If you have a venue in mind that doesn't have or offer full-service amenities, such as a beautiful park, historic home, or your own backyard, don't despair. You can bring in everything you need. Many people actually think do-it-yourself parties are more cost-effective. That is not always true. After hiring and paying the caterer; and renting a tent, chairs, tables, linens, china, silver, glassware, heater or air-conditioner, and even the dance floor and rest rooms, you may be paying even more than what some of the fanciest hotels charge. Remember too that you or someone you hire will need to be in charge of orchestrating every last detail. So when you have your heart set on stringing lights up in your parents' garden or your daughter falls in love with a hip but very empty loft, you need to decide if this perfect site is worth the extra effort and if you are up to the task (or willing to pay an event planner to tend to the details; SEE PAGE 48). Even if you have very involved family and friends, such as a mother who's an amazing chef and has offered to whip up the meal, you need to consider if you have enough kitchen space for her to prepare appetizers, entrees, and desserts for your entire guest list or if you will have to rent more facilities. And if you do, it's not likely you will have enough place settings for all your guests; you will have to bring in those too. That said, some of the best parties have been at a family home—time and again.

Getting Okays

Really, the only thing that may hamper the plans for a particular site are official okays, either from the town if you want a park or beach (be sure to research permits and insurance riders) or from the location's own rules. Some historic sites, for instance, have limited electrical capabilities that may not be prepared for ultra-modern deejay equipment or they may require that your band bring in extra gear, which is a cost that gets passed on to you. Or if you are considering your backyard, find out if your town has laws about loud music after certain hours or parking on your street.

When choosing a location, there are ways to be cost conscious. While there is little you can do about the date if it coincides with your child's birthday, it's good to know that most venues charge higher fees during spring and summer months when other events like weddings are very popular. The same is true during Christmas and New Year's when spots book up well in advance for holiday parties. And no matter the time of year, Saturday evenings are typically the priciest. Still, you can find ways to cut costs. If a location you want is booked for a Saturday night, ask if you can hold an afternoon event there instead. Often banquet managers will want to book any open spots and be willing to negotiate the price. The same is true for Sunday; if they have a morning or afternoon event booked, find out about a twilight party (five or six o'clock) or ask about a brunch if the site is booked for later in the day.

When you start scouting locations, keep these points in mind. Spend time with the banquet or catering manager; he needs to be accommodating, amenable, and available to answer any of your questions or concerns now and through the day of your function. Make sure you like the person and feel that you could work well together.

The place needs to be spacious enough for your guests when they are sitting at tables eating as well as when they are up milling about and dancing. But you don't want to end up in a spot that's too big for your crowd either. Too much room will leave you with huge gaps between tables and a dance floor that feels unused even when the whole party is up on their feet. Take a look at the carpet and other furnishings already in place. Although you are not going to live there, you still need to make sure they work with your notions for a color scheme and theme. Find out if any pieces that don't fit the bill can be moved or stashed out of the way for the duration of your party. Look at window treatments or murals; they might make the beginnings of a wonderful theme (Venetian, beach, retro) and might be the perfect background for formal pictures. Also look around for flowers, plants, lights, and other decorations. Ask if they are standard or are set out for another function. If you like them, using them may be a way to save on your decorating budget. If you don't, inquire whether or not they can be moved.

Hiring an Event Planner

A party planner's role can be big or small—she may oversee every detail and function as the coordinator of the rest of your team of professionals, or she may simply be on hand to pitch in on the day of the event. At first, many think that hiring such a professional is quite extravagant but those who have done it attest that doing so is well worth the expense. (FOR MORE, SEE "CONSIDERING AN EVENT PLANNER," PAGE 48.)

Working with the Caterer

If you will be using an on-site caterer, the task of finding one is taken care of. If you will be looking for a freelance caterer, start meeting with some in the beginning planning stages, at least a year ahead of your date, because the best book up quickly. Start by asking friends and family for any recommendations, take note of any events you go to where the food is exceptionally tasty, inquire at your favorite local restaurant, and talk to other party professionals, especially at your location, about whom they recommend. When you meet with the caterer, find out how willing they are to work with menus geared to both kids and adults. Make sure, if you want two different menus, that they understand that and are willing to work within those parameters. Also inquire whether the caterer has experience with kosher menus and food preparation if that will be your desire. While you don't have to be fast friends, be sure you get along enough to work with them well. Ask to see portfolios and menu selections to get an idea of style, creativity, and what to expect. If you are considering a buffet, ask to see shots of setups; for plated meals, check out the overall presentation to get a sense of the caterer's style. Find out if the caterer offers menu tastings—most do. You and your child should both attend. Expect a range of dishes; there should be an hors d'oeuvre or two, an appetizer, entree, side dish, and dessert.

In addition to all the kitchen preparations that need tending to, there are many more details the caterer will be charged with, including supplying trained wait staff, table setup and settings, stocking and working the bar, and more. So whether you end up using an on-site caterer or one you hire from outside, it's important to know that you and the caterer should be discussing not only menu possibilites but also table details, the number of wait staff allotted for your party, and reception and service styles.

Making the Menu

Choosing or creating a menu for a bat mitzvah is perhaps the most tricky part of the party planning, since the kids probably will not eat what the adults do nor do the adults always like what the kids do (although you'd be surprised how much the grown-ups go for the kids' fare). And somehow you and your caterer need to please both sets of guests and be smart about your budget while doing so. There is no reason to serve pricey filet mignon for all when your child's friends would be much happier with grilled burgers and fries. And while most adults enjoy sitting down and taking the time to appreciate a delicious meal, kids don't typically stay seated more than a minute. That's why Ilene Rosen, savory chef at The City Bakery in New York City, always recommends buffets. "Children don't want to stay still," she says. "They

are always walking around, moving, grazing, and discovering different things." That doesn't mean that a children's menu should be uninspired; it can be great fun as well as creative and delicious. It does, however, need to be appropriate. Laurence Craig, owner of Laurence Craig Distinctive Celebrations in Maplewood, NJ, likes buffets for their versatility. "A buffet allows for several things that a seated, served meal does not. First off, we can satisfy the meat eaters and the vegetarians with ease," he says. "And allergies and dietary restrictions are easily taken care of." In addition to the food choice a buffet caters to, Craig also says that a buffet can be as much of a focal point as any centerpiece is. And since many buffets are vast, making a statement in the space, treat them as you would any other display. Stack serving pieces to make sculptures and choose colorful garnishes and ingredients. Decorate with related props or fruits, vegetables, and flowers—be careful that any flowers used are edible and free from pesticides (your caterer should be aware of this information or be able to get the necessary answers). If flowers are set on or near any food, then guests will assume they can eat them, and they will. Or, have the florist work with your caterer to produce arrangements that fit in at each station and with the rest of the room. Ask to go through the caterer's sample menus for both kids and

menu makeup

It is fun to be creative with what you serve, but it is also equally important to know your audience. A well traveled group of guests may be eager to try new and **different dishes** that wouldn't fly with a more "steak and potatoes" crowd. And while kids are sophisticated these days, you still want to keep their menu **easy to please**. It is always safe to go with tried-and-true favorites like made-to-order pizza bars, pasta stations, make-your-own **salad stations**, sushi bars, barbeque night, Chinese noodle stations, and build-a-burger bars to name a few. (CHECK OUT SOME CREATIVE MENUS ON PAGE 73.)

BUFFET SET
Make the buffet line
move smoothly by
pre-pairing forks and
knives. Bind with
ribbon and set in
container adorned
with complementing
ribbon. Tie spoons on,
too, or set nearby.

adults from other functions or ask the caterer to create a suggested menu for your party (FOR SAMPLE MENU IDEAS, SEE PAGE 73). Help form ideas by providing any thoughts you or your child have, some favorite foods, or any themes you are considering. There might also be a crowd-pleasing family dish that can inspire the caterer or be recreated. Dessert activities are also popular at these events, and although they are mainly for the kids, the adults have been known to join in the fun. Find out if the caterer can offer out-of-the-ordinary desserts, like make-your-own sundae bars, snow cones, and cookie-decorating stations (FOR MORE DESSERT IDEAS, SEE PAGE 68).

Buffet versus Seated

Discuss reception service style with the caterer; what you decide may affect the menu. Buffets with stations are popular with kids because they offer the most flexibility in dish choice. But you don't want to be creative with everything. Some kids are adventurous while others are finicky, so make sure you've got some of the standards in place and go wild in other areas of the party planning. For the adults, choose between a buffet or a seated meal. For a buffet-style meal, find out if it will be set up in a different room or how it will be separated from the kids' meal. Otherwise there will be confusion, unnecessarily long lines, and the guests will end up with the wrong food on the wrong plates.

"Take advantage of the decorating benefit a buffet brings to a room," says Craig. "Buffets allow for a beautiful visual presentation." Also, notes Craig, "When dozens of children swarm a buffet, it can be demolished in seconds, rendering it unappetizing for the adults." But no matter where you set up, Craig offers this rule of thumb. "There should be one buffet line or station for every forty to fifty guests."

Catering fees are typically charged per person and vary depending on the region of the country, time of day, day of the week, time of year, formality of the event, number of guests, menu selection, and style of service. Often, seated meals are pricier since they are more formal in nature, requiring more courses, fancier food, and a larger wait staff. It is a misconception, though, that buffets are always less expensive. Certainly the wait staff, even if there are multiple manned serving stations, may be more minimal, but depending on the menu selection, buffets can be as expensive as the most elegant seated meal. And since guests often help themselves at buffets, it is hard to know exactly how much food to order, even for the kids. "Even if kids don't eat or just take a bite," notes Rosen, "they definitely fill their plates." Certainly, caterers have the experience to make an educated guess, but it will never be exact so you usually end up spending a bit more to ensure there is enough for all. Sometimes hiring staff to serve each item in a buffet line saves time and money.

REFRESHINGLY
PRETTY

Colorful drinks with
festive garnishes bring
an element of fun to
any party. Make drinks
available in alcoholic
and non-alcoholic so
everyone gets to enjoy.

Working the Bar

The bar is also handled by the caterer or banquet manager. Bar service is not just about what to stock, how to set up, and what to serve. These are important points, but the most noteworthy issue is, once again, how to make it work for both kids and adults. Because while you want to give a choice of drinks to the adults, there is absolutely no alcohol to be served to the kids. There is, of course, the option of not serving liquor at your function at all. If that is not appealing, then be sure you tell the caterer or banquet manager who should have strategies in place to assure that the children will not have access to alcohol. One idea is to set up bars at opposite sides of the room or even in separate rooms so there is really no reason for any of the younger set to be at the grown-up bar. There is also the notion of "ID" type bracelets for the kids so the bartenders don't serve anyone who is wearing one. Really, though, says Victoria Dubin, event planner and designer in Purchase, NY, "your caterer has the experience to be on top of it. Many even have security people in place specifically to monitor this type of situation."

There are a few different ways to plan for and stock a bar. A fully-stocked open bar is virtually limitless in drink choices and is also the costliest. If you choose this style, but are watching your budget, consider house-brand liquors instead of top-shelf brands, or bringing in your own from a liquor wholesaler. Be sure to ask if the caterer allows liquor to be brought in and if they charge a corkage fee (a price for every bottle opened when it's not their own). Another choice is to ask the caterer to close the bar an hour or so before the event ends—a bonus is that people stop drinking well before they have to drive home. A wine bar complete with a selection of reds, whites, and champagne is festive; add some beer, too. It's trendy and cost effective to have the caterer or bartender create a signature cocktail; perhaps something to go with a theme or one from a favorite place. You can serve that rather than offer an open bar. So everyone can share in this specialty drink, have the bartenders make it with and without alcohol. Since there are always a few kids, no matter how much you discourage it, who will try to sneak a drink, try to avoid this as much as possible by setting them up with their own cool drinks. A soda bar is always popular as is a selection of colorful frozen drinks served in funky glasses and garnished just so. Fresh fruit perched on glass edges are simple and chic—a fruit kabob transforms a basic drink into a tropical treat. In addition, try colorful sugared swizzle sticks. Use just one or a few for a striped sensation. And you can always request that the bartender mix up some non-alcoholic versions of favorite grown-up drinks, like daquiris, margaritas, and piña coladas.

CAKE AND
CANDLES
A beautifully
decorated cake
becomes the center-
piece of a party,
long before the
candlelighting begins.

Selecting a Cake

Forget the idea of a simple birthday cake. After all, the cake at an event like this is a showpiece, one to be admired by guests and to be used later as the center-piece of the candlelighting ceremony (SEE PAGE 68). Maybe then—and only maybe—will the cake be sliced and served. Some find that with so many other dessert possibilities (SEE PAGE 68), the cake isn't necessary. But what is a birthday party without one? Today, cakes can be made into any shape, size, color, or design. They can be tiered or flat, match a theme or even a swatch of fabric from the bat mitzvah girl's dress. And they can be embellished with myriad edible details made of sugar, marzipan, chocolate, and more.

Don't expect your typical frosted confection if you are going for a couture cake. "Rolled fondant or gum paste is best to cover the cake," says Elisa Strauss, owner of Confetti Cakes in New York City, "rather than frosting." Fondant and gum paste produce a flat, matte surface, and can be made to match any color, which makes it ideal for decorating. And, says Strauss, "you get the most realism with it because you can achieve the best details." Strauss suggests that when meeting with a cake designer, bring in any inspirational photos, ideas about a theme, swatches, and even the invitation so he or she can get an idea of color and style.

If the cake will be just for the candlelighting, don't order one to feed everyone. Since most cake designers charge per person to determine how big to make the cake, it seems like a waste to make an enormous cake no one may get the chance to eat. "Order a smaller cake that is a pre-sentable size for display and the ceremony," suggests Stephen Maronian, owner of Sweet Lisa's Exquisite Cakes in Greenwich, CT, "and take it home to serve at the brunch the next day. It is also more cost-effective," says Maronian. That way, "you are not paying for what you don't need and you can put more money into the cake design." You can even ask a cake designer to make a dummy cake, which is really just foam shapes that have been expertly decorated to look like a cake. Or, you can split the cake, making half dummy and half real to serve just the kids cake. Although sometimes that well-intentioned plan doesn't go as planned. "Once the adults see kids eating it," says Strauss, "they usually want some too." And be forewarned, a dummy cake might make less waste but is not always less expensive. "A dummy cake can cost as much as a real one," notes Maronian.

When you do want cake for dessert, there are a variety of scrumptious choices and combinations. Most bakers offer specialty choices as well as the standards. And standard does not mean ordinary, either. Bakers just find that these are what people truly like. Many will also

MORE DESSERT

In addition to cake, you might want to serve other kinds of dessert. The choices are equally tasty to eat and see, such as fresh fruit tarts.

try to accommodate special requests. For cake layers, there are vanilla, chocolate, carrot, lemon, banana, marble, and hazelnut. Filling choices include buttercream in flavors from vanilla and chocolate to almond, praline, espresso, and mocha. There are cream cheese frostings, chocolate ganache, and citrus curds too. The icing on top can be fondant or gum paste, buttercream or ganache. Maronian will frost the cake with a thin layer of buttercream or ganache, then cover it with fondant or marzipan to make the decorating clean and easy.

With so many choices it can be difficult to decide. Plan a tasting with the cake designer. Expect to taste a few different cakes, fillings, and frostings. If you have already booked the designer, there should be no extra charge for a formal tasting. Go about finding the cake designer just as you would any other professional. Talk to family and friends and make a note of any confection you see or taste that you like. Talk to your caterer and event planner too; undoubtedly, they will have the name of a favorite cake decorator to share.

One of the most important questions to ask a potential cake designer, says Strauss, is if the cake is made from scratch. The look is important, but so is the taste. She also advises getting a sketch of your cake and a "well-detailed cake agreement." This contract should state the cake flavor and filling, the color and type of frosting, how many embellishments, what kind, what color, and what ingredients and its size. That is the best way to avoid any confusion. And don't forget to ask your baker what else they can bring to the party. Strauss is known for her fancy cupcakes. Maronian will bake cookie place cards, favors, and even table numbers.

Deciding on Desserts

Even if your son or daughter wants a cake for dessert, that's probably not all you should serve. Today, desserts have become activities themselves, whether the guests are engaged in making their own at a special station, at their table, or with a professional who can wrap the goods to go. And all this is not just for the kids; sometimes the adults have just as much fun partaking in the festivities. Some ideas include ice cream bars complete with a variety of flavors—hard, soft-serve, or both—and toppings; chocolate fondue; an all-chocolate table with chocolate mousse, cake, cookies, brownies, and more; a cookie decorating station; old-fashioned snow cones with a machine and server; a smoothie station; a mini tart selection; and fresh fruit.

Coordinating the Candlelighting

This ceremony has no religious significance but has come to be a well-observed tradition at bar mitzvah parties everywhere as a way of recognizing family and

friends. Thirteen candles, typically long, slender tapers, might illuminate the "birthday cake," be set in a candelabra, or be placed in individual candleholders that rest on a table festooned with the cake, flowers, or other decorations. Since the cake is often tied into the theme of the day or is just a beautiful and artistic confection, the bar mitzvah family may decide to have the cake set out during the course of the party. To ensure it is kept intact and out of harm's way, the cake may be displayed in a spot that's out of the way but still visible enough to be appreciated by all. Then, when the time comes, the cake can take center stage. It may be placed on the dance floor or other central location where everyone can get a glimpse of the happenings. And instead of the focus being on blowing out the candles, the emphasis is on lighting the candles. Each person or group of people called upon to light one is special to the bar mitzvah child in some way.

Just how the honorees are called up can be as involved as choosing who will light each candle. Typically grandparents, aunts, uncles, and cousins are included as are parents and siblings. School friends, camp friends, special teachers, and family friends may also be called upon to light a candle. Depending on how many people your child wants to call, he can group certain people together; for example, all his camp friends or a group of cousins can share one candle. Many cele-

brants write down simple thoughts to share about each candlelighter and why they are important in the child's life. Other kids jazz up the ceremony a bit and write poems for each honoree. There are even professionals who will collect all the pertinent information and then write the poems for the bar mitzvah child. Others compose songs, tell funny stories, or just simply call everyone up for a hug and a kiss. Some folks have the photographer or videographer create a slide show or video montage (SEE CHAPTER EIGHT, GETTING THE PICTURE) to run prior to or just after the candlelighting. It is actually the perfect time to run the video, when everyone is already gathered together in one place. People will have the chance to focus on this part of the celebration without other distractions.

The candlelighting typically takes place after the main meal has been served, and everyone is expected to take their seats while it is happening. Any side entertainment should be shut down at this time and music stopped (SEE CHAPTER SEVEN, THAT'S ENTERTAINMENT). Because kids have a hard time staying put for long, try to keep candlelighting short and fast paced, no more than twenty minutes at the most.

After the celebrant honors family and friends, it is his parents' turn to honor him. In a short speech, parents welcome guests and thank them for coming, then turn their attention to their child. Speeches are often funny,

THE CANDLE LIGHTING

In this ceremony, friends and family are recognized by the bat mitzvah child on her special day. Candles can be set in decorative holders, a candelabra, or around a cake.

anecdotal, cheery, reminiscent, and can get emotional. If you prefer, a video montage or slide show can be shown here with pictures of your child from birth until the present. Try to use a mix of shots including some from home, vacation, camp, studying, playing, and with friends and family.

Seating the Guests

You might have tables for the adults only, letting the kids hang out in a kids' club or lounge tucked away on the other side of the room. Or you may do tables for both adults and kids, keeping the party all in one place. Either way, deciding who sits where is like a puzzle that takes time and dutiful consideration to make all the pieces fit just right. You want the mix of people at each table to be the best it can be and guests to feel like they're in a special place, no matter where they are ultimately assigned. Start early but don't expect any final charts right away. You will be tweaking assignments until the very end.

If you will use the tables provided by your location, know that standard tables fit anywhere from eight to twelve people. Depending on your site, the tables might be smaller. Ask your caterer or banquet manager for a table diagram to get a sense of how tables are set up to fit in the space. Make sure placement of the dance floor,

kitchen entrance, and closest bathroom access are all marked. Kids like being seated near the dance floor and don't mind being in close proximity to the band's speakers, unlike many adults who find loud music blasting next to them a nuisance and unpleasant indeed. Elderly guests or parents of very young ones might appreciate sitting near the door closest to the bathroom. These are all important points to keep in mind when initially planning your seating. And, before you actually do put pen to paper, make multiple copies of the blank diagram so you don't get bogged down with all the changes you will inevitably make. Another idea is to get a few stick-on notepads and write each guest's name on a sheet of paper. This way you can switch names around continuously until you find the perfect arrangement.

Family Tables

Start with the table at which you will sit. An adult family-only table is one way to go and depending on the size of your family, may require an entire table. This is especially lovely if family members have traveled a great distance just for the occasion and you can enjoy a little more time together. Otherwise, divide the family democratically so as to not hurt feelings, spreading grandparents, favorite aunts, uncles, and cousins over several tables but in close proximity to your table. For divorced parents, depending on the situation, you can all sit

together or, if everyone will be more comfortable seating apart, you can arrange separate adult family tables.

Kids' Tables

In every effort to make the bar mitzvah child the center of the celebration, many families choose to set up one long table, banquet-style, with the bar mitzvah child seated at the center of one side or at the head. If you do a kids' lounge, as many people do, there might be cafe or bistro tables, sofas or bar stools. If so, no assigned tables or seats are necessary as kids will grab a chair just for a moment or two to eat. If you will have lots of small tables instead, keep kids' tables concentrated in one area. Certainly all of the kids won't be able to sit at the celebrant's table, but they should all feel like they are as close as they can be. In terms of the bat mitzvah child's table, she should be able to choose who sits with her, unless you have a strong feeling that a sibling, cousin, or family friend should be in the mix. If so, discuss this with your child and explain your reasoning. Remind her that not all her friends are going to be able to be seated together, so it's important that everyone have at least one person they know well at their table. The last thing you want is a sad group because someone is feeling left out.

Adult Tables

As for your friends, seat couples together and try to group some friends and relatives. You might want to try to mix it up too; it can make for lively and interesting banter. Be considerate of friends or relatives who have children at the party: If the children are old enough to sit by themselves, seat them with other little ones at a table next to their parents. On the other hand, parents with older kids in tow might appreciate some distance from their kids, and vice-versa. They'll surely find each other when they need to.

Finalize your seating chart as much as possible about three weeks or so before the event (SEE "TABLE SEATING WORKSHEET," APPENDIX, PAGE 139). That way you or a calligrapher will have time to write out table cards (also called escort cards) with each guest's name and assignment. It's proper to coordinate these cards with other event stationery such as invitations and menu cards (SEE CHAPTER FIVE, INVITATIONS AND MORE). Table cards are flat or tented and come in a variety of styles and colors. Married couples' names are written on one card together; families seated at the same table may go on one card or parents can be written on one, children on the other, or each child may get his own card. All set out, these cards can make a beautiful display. An alternative to cards, if you and your child want to infuse the party with something beyond the traditional, is a scroll, written in calligraphy with names and table assignments and attended to by a member of the wait staff. Each guest presents his name, which the attendant finds on the scroll, and is then escorted to his table by another member of the wait staff.

a mix of menus

Here is a fun and festive selection from two top caterers. Of course, any of these dishes or those from your own caterer can be adjusted to suit kosher and other dietary needs.

From Ilene Rosen of The City Bakery

State Fair fried chicken corn dogs corn-on-the-cob cornbread macaroni and cheese **Make-Your-Own Mexican** (an interactive station) **fish tacos** quesadillas with an intriguing array of fixings: **beans, steak, chicken, cheese, onions, peppers, tomatoes, cilantro, jalapeño** chips, salsa, and guacamole **jicama and mango salad** Winter Chill beef stew classic mashed sweet potatoes egg noodles biscuits **Indian Flavor** chutneys **breads: nan, papadum, paratha** chicken curry **basmati rice** green beans with shredded coconut and mustard oil **High Tea Station** tiny tea sandwiches **scones** raspberry jam **crème fraîche** miniature tarts "evening hour" chocolate cookies vanilla bean sugar domes

From Laurence Craig of Laurence Craig Distinctive Celebrations

"Picnic" Buffet molasses BBQ chicken tart **mini Reubens** hot dogs in "straight jackets" with honey mustard grandma's potato latkes Nova Scotia "cones" with scallion cream cheese **Fun Finger Food** coconut chicken with duck sauce **four cheese pizza rolls** fried mozzarella ball kebabs **stuffed buffalo wings with hot sauce** jumbo pretzels with cheese sauce **X-treme Cuisine** devil's chicken with wild cherry and chile jelly glaze roasted turkey chili with jalepeño "poppers" Thai curry noodles with peanuts, basil, and chives **roasted salmon fillet and kimchee with citrus pepper oil** poblano-butter roasted sweet corn

5

INVITATIONS AND MORE

IN THIS CHAPTER

- invitation wording

- the printing process

- working with a calligrapher

Stationery is much more than just an artful presentation of the facts. It is a series of correspondence and cards documenting the event. Stationery is used to announce an event, invite, direct, guide, and thank guests. It offers the first glimpse of the event, introducing the level of formality, theme, and colors; it also provides an appropriate format for thank-yous in the weeks following. You can even transform other paper elements, such as guest books and sign-in posters into keepsakes. The stationery pieces can be cute, clever, beautiful, whimsical, subtle, or outrageous in style—but most important to remember is that they also need to tell people what they are coming for, where to be, and when to be there.

There are a number of stationery components you will need and all should match or complement each other in design. Don't think, though, that there is any rule against mismatched pieces. But if you are concerned about proper etiquette, those rules dictate that stationery used for the same event should relate well and also be in keeping with the tone of the party. Depending on the type of event and your guest list, you will need all or some of the following: save-the-date cards, ceremony programs, table numbers, escort cards, place cards, menu cards, thank-you notes, and, of course, the invitations themselves and all their parts.

STATIONERY
PIECES

Aside from the invita-
tion, several other
elements make up the
stationery wardrobe.
From top center:
R.S.V.P. and direction
cards; thank-you notes;
envelopes; escort cards.

All the Parts

Invitations come packaged many ways and the components are determined by the style of event and the information you need to relay to guests. In addition to the
actual invitation, there may be a response card, response
envelope (unless your card is a postcard), direction
card, transportation card, and possibly an accommodations card with details about area hotels. Reception
cards are only necessary if just the ceremony points are
printed on the invitation, in which case the reception
card accompanies the invitation and provides all the
details of the reception. Don't forget the outer mailing
envelopes and the slightly smaller inner ones too. "If
you are conserving your budget, don't do all the cards,"
says Julie Holcomb of Julie Holcomb Printers in
Emeryville, CA. "You can easily print some or all of the
information on one card."

Save-the-Date

Many people send save-the-date cards, especially if
friends and family are spread across the country, or even
the world. These cards give people a heads-up about
timing so they can make any necessary travel plans.
They are the first piece of the stationery wardrobe to be
mailed out, should be sent at least six to nine months
before the event, and may provide the first hint at what's
to come. If you don't have a theme, color scheme, or

other decorating ideas in place yet, don't fret. It's more
important to get the word out.

Know that save-the-date cards aren't just for out-of-
town guests. If you live in an area with a large Jewish
population and your child knows at least one or two
other children with the same bar mitzvah date, you can
send save-the-date cards to everyone on the guest list.
Just make sure that whomever you do send them to is
definitely going to be on the final guest list. You don't
want to include those you are not sure of yet, like work
associates, or a new acquaintance you are hoping to
know better. Keep wording brief and simple—it can be
whimsical or formal—but don't give too much away.
This is not the invitation, after all, you just want to let
everyone know that great things are in store and to, well,
save the date.

Invitation Information

On the invitation, include all the pertinent information:
your child's name, that this is his bar mitzvah, the date,
the time, the place, and the address, as well as your
name. Be sure the name and address of the reception
location also appears if it is different from the ceremony
site and you will not be sending a separate reception
card. If there will be transportation provided for the
kids, you may say so on the invitation. You may include
a request for an R.S.V.P. with your address, phone

number, or even e-mail address (depending on how formal the invitation), or use a response card and envelope instead. Years ago, etiquette called for people to respond to an invitation with a handwritten note on their own stationery. This is still preferred by the more socially formal, but should not be expected. Including a response card will likely prompt more timely responses than if your guests are expected to write their own notes. It is also more convenient for guests and can help you keep track of the invitation list.

Response and Direction Cards

There are several variations of a response card. There is the "M-line" card, which is designed just as it sounds, with an upper case "M" followed by a line for the guests to fill in their names and a place to check off whether they "will attend" or "will not attend" and a date before which a reply is requested. Another option is a card that simply states "Kindly respond by" or "Kindly respond before" with a date: This type of card allows guests to write their own note on a supplied card with a pre-stamped and addressed envelope, combining the charm of years past with the convenience of today. A postcard response card is another way to go—guests can fill in their answer (use the "M-line" or "kindly respond") on one side while you have provided your address and a stamp on the other. This route requires little effort on

the guests' parts and is a bit easier to budget since there are no response envelopes and postcard stamps are less expensive than ones for letters.

Direction cards usually have the directions to the synagogue and the reception site written out from several starting points or highways. Maps of a few blocks surrounding your venue are also helpful to print; it's a lot simpler than it sounds since many locations have maps already made up that you can pass along to your stationer or printer. The same is true for the accommodations card; hotels can provide direction information and maps for printing. Even better, some locations and hotels will provide you with pre-printed cards and directions that you can slip right in with the invitation pieces, which will reduce your printing costs. But ask to see these cards first to ensure they are tasteful and in accordance with your invitation style. If not, it might not be worth the money you would save if it doesn't complement or fit well with your other printed pieces.

Color Combos

White and ecru stock with black or gray type is classic for the bar mitzvah invitation. Today, vibrant color combinations are all the rage. Consider with your child any mix of fun color combinations for the paper and ink—take a look at some cool colorful duos on the opposite page.

anatomy of an
invitation

An invitation ensemble might include:

1. outer envelope This is the largest of the invitation envelopes since all the enclosures need to fit inside. The sender's return address is printed on the back flap; guests' names and addresses are handwritten or penned by a calligrapher on the front.

2. inner envelope If used (typically only with formal invitations), this slightly smaller envelope is stuffed with the invitation and other enclosures. Addressed with the guests' names (more informally than on the outer envelope) and left unsealed, it is placed directly inside the outer envelope. **3. invitation** Traditionally the invitation is a flat, single-paneled card with writing on the front side only. Sometimes Hebrew lettering is included. More modern invitations may be round or square, open cards, or even booklets with photographs of the bar mitzvah child. For invitation wording suggestions, see page 82.

4. reception card This card is not a necessary part of the invitation ensemble, but may be included when reception information is not printed on the invitation, whether for space reasons, style, or if some guests will be asked only to the ceremony or to the reception. This piece should match the other stationery pieces design-wise. Additional cards for travel and accommodations, bus transportation, and maps with driving directions can also be created and are typically this size. **5. response card (or response post-card)** Another diminutive card, this piece is provided for the convenience of guests. It provides an easy way for them to let hosts know whether they will or will not be attending. See page 85 for different wording styles. **6. response card envelope** Just big enough for the response card to fit, this envelope is mailed back by the guests to the hosts. The envelope is stamped, the hosts' address is printed on the front, and the back flap is left blank for guests to fill in their own return address.

1

2

3

4

6

5

favorite
ink combinations

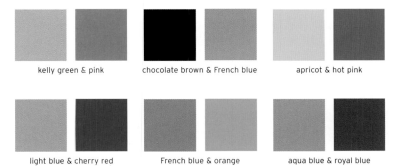

kelly green & pink   chocolate brown & French blue   apricot & hot pink

light blue & cherry red   French blue & orange   aqua blue & royal blue

MAKING THEIR
MARK
As an alternative to a
traditional guest book,
a roll of white art
paper can be stretched
along a table with
buckets of markers
guests use to sign.

Guest List Worksheet

Using the template below, create a worksheet to organize guest details. Add it to your organizer (binder or notebook) since you will want to keep this information readily accessible. You will need to refer to it during the entire planning process, from collecting guests' addresses to noting when thank-yous have been mailed off.

Guest(s) name(s) _____

Address _____

Telephone number _____

E-mail address _____

Number of guests attending _____

Table assigned _____

Gift (or charitable donation) received _____

- ○ Save-the-date card mailed
- ○ Invitation mailed
- ○ R.S.V.P. received
- ○ Other (transportation needed, etc.)
- ○ Thank-you note mailed

For Guests to Sign

Any guest book you select should also complement your stationery style. Set a beautiful storebought book on a table by the reception entrance for guests to sign as they make their way to the tables or consider making one yourself. You can also come up with a creative alternative to traditional books, which makes it fun for the guests to write messages and equally enjoyable for you and your child to savor for the years to come. Some easy and kid-friendly solutions include an oversized poster of your child on which people can write messages, or a roll of white art paper set out with plenty of markers for guests to pen their well wishes. Small cards in the colors of the day can be stacked and left on a table with pens; guests first write their messages, then toss the cards into a large fish bowl or other vessel that has been set out. These notes are fun to go through after the party has ended and can be safely saved away after in a scrapbook, decorative box, or album. You can also tailor-make guest books for each table: Make or buy small books and on each page write—or have your calligrapher write—the name of each guest seated at the table. This gives each guest a chance to have his or her own private page and the result is as many books in a collection as you have guest tables.

You were awesome!
Hope I sound as good
as you did . . .
Love,
Isabelle

great job ariella! ♥
xo,
lisa

Congrat. . .

. . .much love!
Aunti Sophie

SIGN IN HERE

I'm so excited
for you. Thanks
so much for
having me!
♡ Emma

Ariella,
What a wonderful day.
You should be so proud.
Best wishes,
The Abrams family

Ariella You Rock!
Congratulations . . .

Invitation Wording

Invitation language can be traditional, formal, casual, or somewhere in between. It can include only ceremony information, ceremony as well as reception specifics, and even spell out the details of where and by when to respond. Transportation information can also be provided on the invitation or sent on a separate card (as can the R.S.V.P. too). Use standard phrasing, fine tune it to suit your style or level of formality, or work with your child to compose your own. An invitation with original text can be especially heartfelt and meaningful. Typically the parents are introduced as the hosts of the event. Sometimes parents choose to step aside and allow their children to take over that role on the invitation, but still "sign" their names on the bottom. Depending on circumstances, divorced parents may both have their names on the invitation or just one. In the event of a deceased parent, it is proper to include only the name of the parent who is living and to honor the deceased parent in any number of ways during the event.

The most formal language, including the phrase "request the honor of your presence…" is typically reserved for formal weddings and other gala affairs, although some lovely bar mitzvah invitations are written with this request. Following are a few other examples:

TRADITIONAL

MR. AND MRS. JONATHAN STEIN
WOULD BE HONORED TO HAVE YOU SHARE IN PRAYER
AS THEIR SON
Adam Jacob
IS CALLED TO THE TORAH AS A BAR MITZVAH
SATURDAY, OCTOBER EIGHTH
TWO THOUSAND AND FIVE
AT TEN O'CLOCK IN THE MORNING
TEMPLE EILAT
BROOKFIELD, PENNSYLVANIA

Luncheon to follow immediately after the service

INFORMAL

IT WOULD BE WONDERFUL IF YOU CAN BE THERE
WHEN OUR SON **ADAM JACOB**
IS CALLED TO THE TORAH
AS HE CELEBRATES HIS BAR MITZVAH
SATURDAY, OCTOBER 8, 2005
AT 10:00 A.M.
TEMPLE EILAT
BROOKFIELD, PENNSYLVANIA

NIKKI AND JONATHAN STEIN

TRADITIONAL

MR. AND MRS. JONATHAN STEIN

WOULD BE PLEASED TO HAVE YOU JOIN THEM

WHEN THEIR SON

ADAM JACOB

IS CALLED TO THE TORAH

AS A BAR MITZVAH

SATURDAY, OCTOBER EIGHTH

TWO THOUSAND AND FIVE

AT TEN O'CLOCK IN THE MORNING

TEMPLE EILAT

BROOKFIELD, PENNSYLVANIA

luncheon to follow immediately after the service

WITH RECEPTION INFORMATION

PLEASE JOIN OUR FAMILY WHEN

Andrew Jacob

BECOMES A BAR MITZVAH

SATURDAY, OCTOBER EIGHTH

TWO THOUSAND AND FIVE

AT TEN O'CLOCK IN THE MORNING

TEMPLE EILAT

BROOKFIELD, PENNSYLVANIA

CELEBRATE WITH US IN THE EVENING

AT SEVEN O'CLOCK AT

THE HILLS CLUB

333 CEDAR ROAD

BROOK, PENNSYLVANIA

Nikki and Jonathan Stein

Valet parking provided
Festive dress

INFORMAL

WE HOPE YOU WILL JOIN US

WHEN OUR SON

ADAM JACOB

IS CALLED TO THE TORAH

AS A BAR MITZVAH

SATURDAY, OCTOBER 8, 2005

AT 10:00 A.M.

TEMPLE EILAT

BROOKFIELD, PENNSYLVANIA

NIKKI AND JONATHAN STEIN

WITH R.S.V.P. INFORMATION

We hope you will join us
on this special day
when our son
Adam Jacob
becomes a bar mitzvah
Saturday, October eighth
Two thousand and five
at ten o'clock in the morning
Temple Eilat
Brookfield, Pennsylvania

Nikki and Jonathan Stein

Please respond
6 Maple Road
Brookside, Pennsylvania 12345
or e-mail at: rsvp@steins.com

With love and pride
we invite you to share in our happiness
as our son
ADAM JACOB
becomes a bar mitzvah
Saturday, October eighth, Two thousand and five
at ten o'clock in the morning
Temple Eilat
Brookfield, Pennsylvania

Nikki Levine and Jonathan Stein

THE CELEBRATION CONTINUES
WITH A LUNCHEON IN ADAM'S HONOR AT
THE HILLS CLUB
333 CEDAR ROAD
BROOK, PENNSYLVANIA

PLEASE JOIN OUR FAMILY
WHEN OUR SON
ADAM JACOB
IS CALLED TO THE TORAH
AS A BAR MITZVAH
SATURDAY, OCTOBER EIGHTH
TWO THOUSAND AND FIVE
AT TEN O'CLOCK IN THE MORNING
TEMPLE EILAT
BROOKFIELD, PENNSYLVANIA

Nikki and Jonathan Stein

Transportation to the luncheon
will be provided

My family and I would like you
to share in our happiness
as I celebrate my bar mitzvah
Saturday, October eighth
Two thousand and five
at ten o'clock in the morning

Temple Eilat
Brookfield, Pennsylvania

Adam Jacob Stein

ALTERNATIVE WORDING FOR INVITATION OPENERS:

We invite you to share in our joy . . .
We invite you to honor a beautiful tradition . . .
Please share in our happiness . . .
Nikki and Jonathan Stein request your company . . .

SAVE-THE-DATE CARD

SAVE THE DATE

Adam Stein's bar mitzvah
Saturday, October 8, 2005

Morning service begins 10:00 A.M.
Evening celebration
Invitation to follow

R.S.V.P. CARD

M_____
will _____ attend
Adam's friend _____ will need transportation
to The Hills Club.

Please respond by September 17

TRANSPORTATION CARD

ADAM STEIN

Bus transportation will be provided for Adam's friends
from Temple Eilat to The Hills Club.
The bus will depart promptly at 12:30 P.M. from the
synagogue. Please make arrangements to be picked
up at The Hills Club, 333 Cedar Road, Brook,
Pennsylvania at 5:00 P.M.

R.S.V.P. CARD VARIATION

Kindly respond on or before September 17

PLEASE JOIN OUR FAMILY WHEN
...Michael
BECOMES A BAR MITZVAH
SUNDAY, THE THIRTIETH OF NOVEMBER
TWO THOUSAND AND THREE
AT ONE O'CLOCK

TEMPLE EMANU-EL
FIFTH AVENUE AT SIXTY-FIFTH STREET
NEW YORK CITY
(...photographs, please)

Reception to Follow
THE LOTOS CLUB
5 EAST 66TH STREET

BENJAMIN DANIEL AND WILLIAM

---

we invite you to share
...a special day in our lives
as we proudly celebrate
our daughter

alice melanie
עליזה חנה

*** reception ***
dinner and dancing
seven o'clock

woodholme country club
300 woodholme avenue
baltimore, maryland

...lack tie

JOIN US IN
...ING OUR SON
...ER ANDREW
...IS CALLED TO THE TORAH
...A BAR MITZVAH
...AY, THE THIRTY-FIRST OF
...NUARY
TWO THOUSAND AND FOUR
AT NINE FORTY-FIVE IN THE MORNING
TEMPLE SHAARAY TEFILA
BEDFORD CORNERS, NEW YORK
LUNCHEON TO FOLLOW
MERYL AND STEPHEN JACOBS

We ...vite you to share our joy wh... our son
Aaron Michael is called to the
Torah as a Bar Mitzvah

Saturday, October 4, 2003
at ...30 in the morning
Central Synagogue
6... Lexington Avenue (at 55th Street)
New York City

Please join us for a luncheon following the
service at Tabla
1... Madison Avenue (at 25th Street)
New York City

Sandra and Marc Freidus

---

please join us
to share our celebration of the bat mitzvah of our daughter

sarah victoria
saturday the fifteenth of february · two thousand three
at ten-fifteen in the morning
temple beth emeth · scottsdale · arizona
reception following the service
5032 east greenway parkway number 872
scottsdale · arizona

stan and jennifer cook

THE INVITATION

These stationery
pieces not only ask
your guests to join you
on this momentous
occasion, but also give
a hint at the festivities
to come, in their for-
mality, theme, color,
and design.

Designing the Stationery

In the past, the look and style of the invitation had nothing to do with the rest of the celebration. "Today, people are including the invitation in the overall design of the event," says Holcomb. Because of that, she says, people are looking for different designs and those that are colorful and fun. It's best, though, to "keep it simple," she adds. You don't want a cluttered invitation. And, notes Holcomb, "it should suit the occasion." The stationery should also reflect your child's personality and style. Be prepared for plenty of decision making; there are a multitude of designs to choose from and as many different price points. You will find varied shaped and sized papers, weights, textures, colors, patterns, motifs, type styles, and more, and there are a number of ways to personalize them all.

Consider your daughter's favorite color or your son's initials or monogram, for starters, or look to your synagogue for ideas. Is it particularly beautiful? Is it known for its spectacular stained glasswork or intricately carved ark? Maybe you could include a rendering of the artistry on the invitation. How about the reception site? Is it decorated with colors you could use on the invitation or patterns that would be fun to repeat throughout? Take your child and spend the afternoon at the library or visiting different bookstores. Look through art books

and catalogs to find ideas for fun or interesting icons; consider images from sports equipment to flowers, fashion to farm animals. Use plain cardstock, folded invitations, or vellum overlaid on stock. Make them big and bold or small and charming. Embellish with bows, use color for the type or edging, or make them square instead of rectangular. Wrap in paper, roll into cylinders, or send them in boxes. Just check on mailing requirements at the post office first. Odd-sized packages might need special treatment. Find out the cost of postage—anything other than a standard letter size will incur an additional fee. That number adds up quickly when you send out a slew of invitations, so it will be necessary to figure that cost into the overall budget.

Working with a Stationer

Where you order stationery depends on the type of service you need. If you consider yourself a low-maintenance type, and aren't looking for something unusual or different, walk into any stationery store and look through the binders on the shelves. These books are provided by various stationery companies to local stores that sell their products and are filled with sample invitations for different celebrations as well as other printed material. There are many styles to choose from and within those styles, a number of variations in color,

A RAINBOW OF
CARDS
When bold colors are
grouped together,
even unembellished
stationery can make an
impact. Here, a spec-
trum of escort cards
is set out for a party
with a color theme.

borders, type, and artwork. Most selections in albums can be customized to a point, says Holcomb. Look at invitations for other types of events and adapt them to yours; mix and match colors, sizes, typefaces, and embellishments, she suggests. Some stores will discount the cost, others only offer full retail prices. Some private stationers represent these same companies and others. These are also stationers who run businesses from their home (likely you can find someone from your congregation who does and might offer discounts to synagogue members). There are also a variety of online and catalog companies that offer a set of standard pieces that can be personalized with color, typeface, and so on.

Then there are private stationers with their own line of cards and invitations. Here you will find room for a bit more creativity. Some companies are rich in tradition and have been in business for decades; others have only recently been started and can be a source of wonderful new ideas. These stationers tend to make even their standard pieces feel original and many will custom design invitations for you.

If you want a unique stationery wardrobe, consider going to a graphic designer or artist to create the pieces. Any artwork, whether computer generated or hand-drawn, can be brought to a printer and turned into stationery. This choice is typically the most expensive, because you are paying for a design before you ever consider the cardstock and printing costs. If you are prepared to spend the money, the results can be truly wonderful. On the other hand, the larger stationery companies who sell their wares through stationery stores and individuals will probably be the least expensive. The cost for stationery from the smaller sources falls somewhere in between. Prices for stationery will also depend on the printing process used, whether engraving, thermography, letterpress, or offset (SEE "PRINTING METHODS," PAGE 91). And if you use just black ink, your costs will remain low. By adding color to the mix (any color can be created in printing by mixing a combination of black, yellow, magenta, and cyan) you should expect to pay more. Two-color printing is less costly than four-color. And printing on both the front and back of the paper will increase the cost as well.

What to Order

When figuring how many invitations to order, there are a few points to consider. First, remember that each invitee does not actually need his or her own invitation: many will be married couples or families. You want to have a few extra invitations on hand to invite some people you would like to have but don't have the room for initially (send these out no later than a month before the date), to account for any lost in the mail that need to be re-sent, or to put in the photo album, frame, or just tuck

Miss Rebecca Cole
Mr. Henry Altman
Miss Katie Shields
Miss Cricket Day
Mrs. Carolina Hearst
Mr. George Captain
Mr. Milton Cohen
Miss Melody Forbes
Mr. Austin Steiner
Mr. Owen Forbes
Mr. Edgar Bates

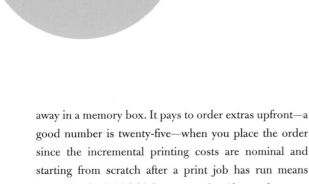

away in a memory box. It pays to order extras upfront—a good number is twenty-five—when you place the order since the incremental printing costs are nominal and starting from scratch after a print job has run means incurring the initial high costs again. Also, order extra envelopes in case of addressing errors. Find out if you can get envelopes earlier than invitations to get a head start on addressing or to send to the calligrapher.

Stationer Contract

Whatever professional you ultimately choose, get the details of the job spelled out in the contract: How many pieces, including names of pieces, the color, style, typeface, color of ink, whether there will be any borders, flourishes, and the like. Many of these details have stock names and numbers; those should be documented as well. If possible, make sure the inventory number of the sample stationery is included. Look for proof instructions (see "proofing"), the date you can expect delivery by, and the cost of additional printings, if necessary.

The Printing Process

Any professional should take you through the whole process, from ordering to printing and delivery. If you work with a freelance artist who does not design invitations as a business, he may refer you to a printer or you might be left to find a printer on your own. In this case, check with other professionals you are working with to see if they can recommend anyone. Ask friends, local restaurants, or hotels who does their menus and stationery, and then look through the Yellow Pages. If you find a printer you like through the phone book, as always, get references. You want the confidence that the invitations will arrive on time and appear exactly as they should.

Proofing

That said, it is always important to recheck all printed details carefully. Leave enough time to change wording, spacing, or even the design, so you do not run into a time or cost problem later. Then, look at a proof of every piece to be printed before the printer runs the job. That means you need to approve an exact copy of all printed material for spelling, accuracy, spacing, centering, and design. Double-check everything. The contract should state no piece will go to press until you sign off on the final proof. If not, write in the clause, even if there is a small charge to revise the proof. It is well worth knowing that your invitation is error free. Expect proofs by fax or e-mail. If they are e-mailed, print them out so you can read them on paper and have someone else look at them too. Clearly mark up any changes and return to the printer or stationer. If you made any changes, make sure to see another proof incorporating those further changes. Check the contract to see if there is any cost for changes made at proof time. Customarily you have one opportunity to make changes, after which you will be charged for any further revisions. There should be no charge if the change is due to the printer's or stationer's error. There may be a charge if you make last-minute changes.

Printing Methods

There are several different types of printing methods used today. Knowing exactly what they are will help determine what you want and what you will be paying for.

Engraving   Engraving is by far the fanciest and most costly. It is an intricate, time-consuming process from the nineteenth century using metal plates etched with die-cut letters. The ink, black or colored, is rolled onto the letters; the paper is then pressed onto the letters to produce raised matte-finished letters on the front and subtle imprints on the back that give the paper a texture you can see and feel. Heavy papers such as cardstock are best to withstand the strong pressure of the engraving process.

Thermography   Thermography is very similar in appearance to engraving, but costs a lot less. In thermography, a powder and wet ink are combined and then heated; as the ink and powder dry together, shiny raised letters are produced. Since there are no plates or pressing involved, the back remains unmarked. For thermography, the choice in paper is limited to smooth stocks since any texture can hamper proper setting of the ink-powder combination.

design elements

Think of any or all of these when creating the invitation.

Paper stock
Typeface Type size
Ink color
Color combinations
Borders Motifs
Hebrew lettering
Monograms Artwork
Embellishments
Bellyband Bows
Confetti Flowers
Glitter Grommets
Photographs
Foil stamping
Embossing
Overlays and Liners
Decorative edging
Packaging

CALLIGRAPHY
STYLE
Calligraphers should
offer to show you their
style sheet, which illus-
trates their artistry
and variety.

Letterpress Even older than engraving, this printing process can trace its origins back to the fifteenth century. The raised letters are debossed, or stamped into the paper, resulting in a less structured look that works well with textured paper. Letterpress can be pricey but is typically favored for invitation styles that are modern, fun, and creative—not too formal.

Offset This style is created with rubber inked cylinders that bring type and motifs to paper. It is even less expensive to produce than thermography. Premade invites and stationery items you find on shelves in a store are likely printed this way. This method offers lots of versatility; the style can be chic or casual, fun or formal.

Working with a Calligrapher

There is no sense sending the invitations so thoughtfully picked out and designed in carelessly addressed envelopes. After all, it's actually the envelope everyone will see first. If your handwriting is less than perfect, you might enlist the help of a good friend or relative in addressing the invitations. Or, you could hire a calligrapher to do the job instead. Calligraphers work wonders with pen and ink and when you stand poised to mail these beautiful envelopes, you might almost not want to let go.

Many calligraphers offer both handwritten and computer-generated work. Handwritten calligraphy is more labor intensive and time-consuming than that printed by computer and therefore more costly, so decide what works with your design and budget. At a meeting with a calligrapher, ask to see a style sheet, a compilation of the different scripts in the calligrapher's repertoire. The samples should show a fair amount of letters so you can get a sense of the calligrapher's talent and the flourishes specific to each typeface to help you choose. Ask about fees, availability, and how many clients the calligrapher has at one time. The latter is especially important because everyone has last-minute changes. You don't want a calligrapher who is constantly inundated with those changes and is late with your order or will rush to get them done. In general, it will take two to four weeks to have your invitations back, more if the calligrapher is especially busy. Factor that into your schedule to allow enough time for stuffing and stamping.

Addressing Envelopes

Even if you are using a calligrapher experienced in the etiquette of addressing, how to do it is still important information to know. Outer envelopes for both kids and adults should have the title, first names, and surnames written out—no nicknames. If you know a guest's middle name, include that if you like too. Married and engaged couples as well as couples living together

Mr. and Mrs. Gregory Hicks — BRILL SCRIPT

Mr. and Mrs. Stephen Baxter — VENETIAN SCRIPT

Mr. and Mrs. Thomas Sullivan — ROOK SCRIPT

Mr. and Mrs. Simon Peters — BICKHAM SCRIPT

Mr. and Mrs. James Gerald — ENGLISH SCRIPT

Mr. and Mrs. James Redway — POINTED PEN ITALIC

Mr. and Mrs. Hank Tayama — KECSEG CASUAL

Mr. and Mrs. Thomas Sinclair — ITALIC

Mr. and Mrs. Chris Baxter — BOOKHAND

Mr. and Mrs. Bernard Levinson — MONOLINE CASUAL

Mr. and Mrs. Thomas Franklin — SCRIPT HANDWRITING

Mr. and Mrs. Roger Winslow — UPRIGHT HANDWRITING

should be on one invitation. If they have different last names, the woman's name is written on the first line, the man's name on the line beneath. All street names are spelled out in full as are other details such as post office box, avenue, cities, states, and countries. For formal invitations, house numbers less than one hundred are spelled out. If your invitation is casual, using a numeral is widely accepted.

For inner envelopes, you may use first names without titles and even nicknames. If parents are invited with children under eighteen, include the children's names on the inner envelope; children over the age of eighteen should receive their own invitation. And if you will invite a single guest with an escort, the phrase "and guest" is written next to your guest's name.

Beyond Envelopes

Calligraphers make art out of plain envelopes, and they can also work wonders with designs for the invitations and other stationery pieces. They can create beautiful invitations, place cards, menus, programs, and more. Most will be happy to show you the bevy of materials they have worked on. Be sure to take the time to look through the pieces. Not only will you get a true sense of the calligrapher's style, but this is also another place to gather more wonderful inspiration.

Calligraphy Contract

The contract needs to state price per envelope charges and if you will pay separate prices for inner and outer envelopes, if applicable. Dates for starting and completing the job are key as is the flexibility for last-minute addresses and place cards. Sometimes calligraphers will put a limit on the number of late changes they can accommodate without charging additional fees. Be sure that number sounds reasonable to you. The contract, should also state the color ink to be used. If the calligrapher will create the type or artwork for any piece of stationery, details should be included in the contract, as well as approvals. Since you will not have the luxury of a proof with each envelope it is your responsibility to give the calligrapher a list of names and addresses that has been checked and rechecked twice. Have your child, spouse, or a friend read it over to ensure spellings and addresses are correct.

In the Mail

Invitations should be sent out eight to ten weeks in advance and even earlier if the event is over a holiday or you know there are other people in town celebrating a bar or bat mitzvah on the same day. Ask that people respond back to you no later than three weeks before the event date. That gives people ample time to check their calendars, for you to allow for any stragglers, and to give your caterer and calligrapher a final guest list and count.

Make a chart in a notebook or on your computer of whom you sent invitations to and who responded, as well as whether they will attend or not (SEE "GUEST LIST WORKSHEET," PAGE 80). Get this response list in place before invitations go out; you will be surprised how quickly some people respond and how difficult a task it is remembering every response and where you wrote it down. You may also want to "key" every response card, meaning assign each invitee a number and write that number in tiny pencil marks on a back corner of the response card. This works well if guests forget to include their names on the response card or if you have trouble reading a guest's handwriting.

Postage

Bring one invitation to the post office for weighing and sizing to determine the amount of postage necessary to mail it. The invitation will likely cost more than a standard letter. The post office offers a wide variety of stamps to choose from and you may even find one that matches your theme or color scheme. Ask that the envelopes be hand-stamped rather than machine stamped so they stay as pristine as possible. Make sure that invitations being mailed overseas have correct postage and airmail stickers.

motif ideas

There are plenty of places to find inspiration for a motif or symbol to spruce up your stationery. Here, some ideas:

Animals bird cat dog fish frog horse turtle
Architecture baseball stadium fort house synagogue
Photographs
Hobbies cars dancing painting piano reading writing Seasonal Elements bees butterflies crickets flowers ladybugs leaves snowflakes trees sun
Sports basketball football hockey lacrosse skateboarding skiing tennis Symbols bows flowers hearts monograms religious shapes stars

6

DECORATING, THEMES, AND FAVORS

IN THIS CHAPTER

- setting the tables

- centerpiece ideas

- fun favors

You have found the perfect spot for the party. It's in a fabulous location, with good space, wonderful acoustics, a spectacular view, and it's within your budget. Sounds super, until you start thinking about decorating, lighting, where the tables will go, what the centerpieces will be, where to carve out a kids' area, how to cover the walls, and more. It's a big job to transform that space into a different place, be it another country, a nightclub, the beach, or a winter wonderland. Well, that's where the details come in. They not only make it look marvelous, but they also create the functional elements of the event. Tend to everything yourself if you're so inclined and you have the time and talent, or hire an event decorator to work with you.

FOR RENT

Caterers have a limited
supply of china and
linens. Dress up the
tables and the room by
tapping into party
rental companies.
Chairs (left) can also be
rented or decorated.

Choosing Colors

Some basic decorating selections, like colors, will come naturally from a theme your child has chosen (SEE SIDEBAR FOR MORE ON THEMES, PAGE 111). If this is so in your case, wonderful. That is one less item to deliberate. Otherwise, it is important to note choosing colors is fundamental in your decorating plans and should be done early on since many other decisions and details will depend on the selection. Know too that color might be the only decorating element you need if you are under time and budget constraints. Having a color assignment will make putting together pieces faster and easier.

There are a number of ways to select and use color. Talk to your child about his or her favorite color or color combination. If there is no immediate or compelling answer, look for inspiration. Help your child go through the closet to pick a favorite shirt or pants to see if that generates any ideas. Sometimes a combination of colors or a terrific pattern is the result.

Nature has an amazing way of using color—take a stroll through a garden to see what blooms strike your child's fancy. Or take a trip to an art museum to get an idea of what palettes famous artists use. You and your child might have a favorite grouping of colors that makes you feel excited or happy. Discover that and you are well on your way.

Chairs and Tables

Proper seating is key for the party flow. Seating the right people together is only one part (SEE CHAPTER ONE, FIRST THINGS FIRST; AND "TABLE SEATING WORKSHEET," APPENDIX, PAGE 139); how the chairs and tables are configured and what they look like is another matter entirely. Use furniture to your decorating advantage. Consider any tables and chairs as a blank slate that you can make over to work with your color scheme, theme, or style for the day.

When venues provide their own tables, they are typically large, round ones. You can certainly use those or bring in some of your own to mix it up a bit. Rent smaller round tables, square ones, or rectangular ones. Rent enough for the entire crowd or save on your budget and rent just a few to work in with the tables provided. Or put adults at large round ones and seat the kids banquet-style at one long rectangular table or two. You might even seat all the guests that way—think of a Victorian-era feast.

There's also the notion of no tables for the kids. According to Victoria Dubin, event planner and designer in Purchase, NY, "Kids don't want to sit and wait to be served." There is just too much to do and see. Instead, Dubin suggests "carving out a kids' lounge that's separate from the adult tables. Have a buffet with kid-friendly foods and stools set up at a low bar, bistro tables with chairs or sofas, and ottomans with coffee and side tables."

COLORFUL TEXTURES
Candy is always fun on kids' tables. Here, yummy necklaces adorn washcloth napkins and jelly beans and Kisses add more tasty decoration. Lollipops (left) stand in for flowers on this vibrant table.

That's all you need, she says, for kids who are going to be constantly popping up and plopping down.

A separate kids area also lets the adults enjoy themselves more too. After all, says Grayson Handy of Prudence Designs and Events in New York City, "this is a celebration for the parents too, and their family and friends." Handy says that for every one hundred guests, an average ratio is seventy adults to thirty kids. "So create a cool, hip atmosphere for the kids where they can hang out, play, get entertained, and eat, but also be at an enjoyable distance from the adults. You want to make it convenient." Lounges, club areas, or entertainment rooms for the kids can be made in most locations especially if yours is a succession of rooms (easy) or one big one. Use different furniture pieces, fabrics, decorations, or screens as boundary markers.

If your space can't accommodate separate areas, or you like the feel of everyone seated together, Dubin recommends leaving something fun on the kids' tables to engage them while they are sitting. This can be anything from a whimsical food container, sunglasses, or glow-in-the-dark accessories. Or, another suggestion from Handy is to have two parties: a luncheon for family and friends following the service and a kids-only party at night. The kids' party can be just for them; try a dance or a sports party. "They can go home after the ceremony, change clothes, and have something to look forward to that night." And the expenses don't have to be any higher for two parties than for one, in fact they can even be less.

Table Design

When setting and dressing the tables, Dubin makes kids' tables funkier versions of the adults', but still keeps them sophisticated. "When you give the kids as much respect as the grown-ups," she says, "most will rise to the occasion." Use a theme to generate some decorating and design elements or start with a color or a detail that already exists at your site. Remember that whatever you choose for each table must work within the context of the room and have widespread appeal too. Depending on the size of your guest list, you may have twenty-five tables or more and the repetition of colors and design will change the overall look of the room and set the stage for the event. "If you choose just one color, you can pick it up in everything—flowers, linens, cards—and repeat the details at every table so that people will notice it," suggests Regina Evans of Regina Evans, Inc., a floral and set designer in New York City. "Repetition makes a strong impression," she says. Start from the bottom up, with tablecloths. Or, if you have a good-looking table—metal or painted wood, for instance—think about placemats instead. Most venues stock basic white tablecloths. Changing the color or pattern is an easy and inexpensive way to transform the room, especially if you have a large

NICE NAPKINS

Rented napkins can spice up tables. Back to front: With a ribbon and a rubber-stamped metal-rimmed tag; twine; polka-dot ribbon; silver ribbon attached to a favor box filled with candy.

room with lots of tables, says Handy. Covered all in white "you have lots of big white marshmallows in the room." Instead, he suggests, "throw on a fuchsia or navy cloth to turn the table into a decorative element." In addition to colors, consider different fabrics, patterns, textures, and sizes, and then think about other pieces, like a rattan woven runner or placemats or a silk polka-dot overlay. Look at the other parts of the setting too. Napkins are inexpensive rentals and upgrading them will not go unnoticed. Napkins add color to the place setting when people take their seats, and they are used all throughout the meal, so not only should they look good, but they should also feel good. Always fold or otherwise embellish napkins: secure with a holder, tie with twine or use them as anchors for place cards or tiny favor boxes.

Chargers are another way to add color, dimension, and interest to a table. They come in many colors, finishes, and designs and can work with any decorating ideas you have devised. Certainly those oversized plates are not necessary—the chargers are removed soon after guests are seated and before the first course is served—but they do make a stunning impact. Still, one way to save money is by choosing from the caterer's china supply instead. Most venues offer a choice of beige or ecru china, and according to Handy, "plated foods always look best on simple white plates."

Glassware can add more color to the table and the room. Use colored or tinted glasses or ones with patterns. Tables can be initially set with a variety of glasses or different ones can be brought out by wait staff as needed during the meal. Create interest with different sized and shaped glasses too. High balls and tumblers, wineglasses, flutes, mugs, and martini-style are a few you will find. Mix and match colors and designs according to your decorating criteria and beverages you will be serving.

Find out what linens, china, glassware, serving pieces, display items, candlesticks, or flatware your venue stocks—there is usually a limited selection—then talk to your caterer, party planner, even your florist to see what they have in inventory. For some of her clients, Dubin finds fabric to match a theme or color scheme and has that made into table coverings, backdrops, even upholstery for furniture. Of course, these are all added expenses so if you're handy at sewing... but don't take on more than you can manage. You can also check out what's available at party rental stores. These businesses exist to rent out the very items you need for just one night and will deliver and pick up the goods to and from your location. Expect to find linens, all kinds of tables, chairs, china, flatware, glassware, and display items like vases. At some of these places, or specialty stores and prop houses, you can rent furniture such as stools and sofas, and anything else you may need to make your party perfect, but remember, it's all at a price.

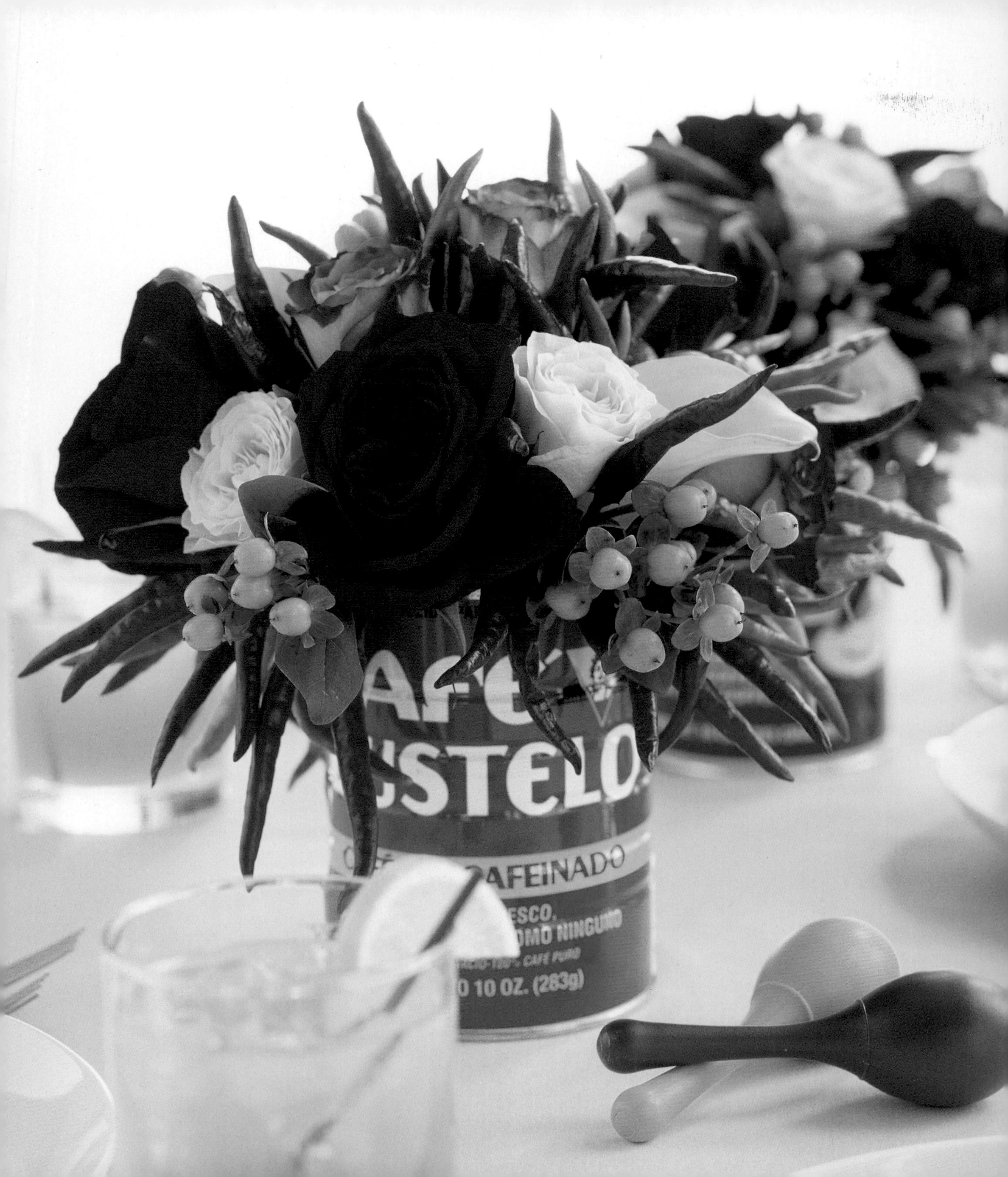
AFÉ
USTELO
AFEINADO
ESCO,
OMO NINGUNO
10 OZ. (283g)

FIESTA FLOWERS

Floral centerpieces can
be anything but tradi-
tional. This arrange-
ment of roses and
rosehips mirrors the
reds and greens of the
colorful coffee can it's
set in. Maracas add to
the festive mood.

Centerpieces

The centerpiece is perhaps the strongest design element of the table setting. It ties in to a color scheme or theme and might project the ideas, sensibilities, and personality of the bar mitzvah child as well. Not all the centerpieces in a location need to be identical, in fact, sometimes it works better when they are not, especially when the displays are different for the kids' tables versus the ones for adults. But all should be linked together somehow and easily co-exist within the room's decor. Centerpieces can be made from practically anything, from flowers to photographs, toy cars to tennis balls. The only thing experts suggest to steer clear of for kids' tables and areas is candles. The potential for disaster is just too great and isn't it better to be safe than sorry?

If you will do floral centerpieces, they can run the gamut from traditional to surprising. If your heart is set on having them tall and grand, just make sure they are very tall so as not to pose a nuisance to guests trying to hold conversations across the table. Or, make them low and lush. Use classic vases or think out of the box and try other containers like buckets, trays, or specialty items. Just don't use anything that might cause a problem if guests take them home, because they will. Florists or floral decorators should have a variety of vessels to choose from or be willing to look for others. If not, you or an event planner can go shopping.

Working with a Florist

When you interview potential florists and floral designers, you want to find someone who has a wealth of ideas, will listen to yours, and who has a sense of style in keeping with yours. Talk to friends and other professionals to get some names, then visit florist shops and showrooms to see the kind of work they do. If you want someone to design and put together arrangements, look for a traditional florist. If you are planning the party yourself, but would like help with the overall aesthetic, consider an event decorator who can coordinate the entire look of your party, including flowers, other centerpiece ideas, table settings, and more decorations.

Walk into a meeting with a florist with some sort of idea or direction of what suits you and your child, the colors you would like to use, and the budget you need to stay within. Be upfront about your numbers from the start; a good floral designer should be able to work with them. It is silly to throw a big number out to see what a designer comes up with and then tell them you were hoping to spend less. There are always ways to trim flower costs and stretch budgets and still make the designs look spectacular. One way to keep costs down is to use flowers in season. They are more readily available and abundant than out-of-season flowers, which may need to be flown in from some exotic locale. Items like pumpkins and gourds work well for fall and sunflowers in metal containers are

MAKE
YOUR
OWN
MEMORIES

CAMERA CLUSTER

A display of artfully
wrapped disposable
cameras is a pretty
centerpiece and is use-
ful too. Guests can
take pictures—collect
them at the end or let
guests take home.

fun for summer festivities. You will pay less for simply constructed arrangements, and a premium for blooms on holidays like Mother's Day and Valentine's Day, when flowers are in high demand.

Florist Contract

Before you book any florists, ask to see samples of their work, both photographs and a real arrangement. Flip through magazines, books, and friends' albums to get a sense of what you like. Coming armed with pictures always helps. Many florists are happy to look at photos you bring to them of arrangements that strike your fancy. Once the florist gets back to you with a proposal of ideas and prices, decide if you want to proceed. If so, have the florist visit the party location, and set up another meeting to discuss specifics of what he thinks works best in the space. Before you sign a contract, make sure it spells out all the details, including the styles of arrangements you are getting, how many, and all the prices. A florist's contract should also include who will set up, and that you expect fresh flowers in full bloom. The contract needs to also indicate if there are any substitutions you won't accept or what the alternative will be if the flowers you agree upon are not available that day. Find out if the florist will pick up other decorative pieces you have rented from him after the event, and by when.

Other than Flowers

Some folks forgo flowers altogether for a particular theme that is carried out through the table settings. For a sports theme, for instance, centerpieces can be "sculptures" of different equipment: one table of football paraphernalia or a grouping of balls, one table of baseball, one of basketball, one of tennis, and so on. The plates and linens would be coordinated to resemble a field or playing court. Certainly lots of guests will think these displays are fun to look at and even more fun to take home. Instead, why not consider donating the equipment to a local boys' and girls' league that would benefit from some new gear. Handy has worked with many families who he says, "are happy to spend the money on their children but are also socially aware. It's very admirable." One party he planned was centered around books, since the bat mitzvah girl was an avid reader. The centerpieces were wonderfully styled book piles—every table had a different genre of titles. After the event, all of the books were donated to underprivileged schools. Donating the goods not only gives back to your community, it also shows children *tzedakah* in action, a concept they have been learning about since the early years of religious school and one that is an important component of any bar mitzvah. If this is your desire, let guests know that the centerpieces are there for them to enjoy at the party but not to take home.

PRETTY PLACE
CARDS

Place cards guide
guests to their
assigned seats. Let
them meet a favor
there too, like this
sugar box with a
sugared daisy on top.

Leave a printed card on the table detailing that the items will be donated and to where. If you fear the card will get lost on the table or you envision a minimal, uncluttered table, print the information on a ceremony program and have the emcee make an announcement during the meal.

Candy is another tool for decorating—and it serves two purposes since it can be used as a giveaway at the end of the night too. Kids go crazy for candy, which is good and bad: You can't go wrong with it, but you want to use it sparingly. For starters, the sugar generates lots of excess energy. And second, kids may be tempted to take apart any centerpiece made solely of candy; filling glass cylinders or clear candy jars with jelly beans, gumdrops, and wrapped candies makes spectacular displays for the table, but ones that are not always practical. If you don't want to risk it, instead, use the treats to embellish a topiary or throw a handful of loose candy on the table as additional decoration. If you do use candy at the table, try to avoid a lot with wrappers, or your pretty table will be a messy scattering of discarded paper. Another benefit to candy: It's easy to find, readily available, very colorful, and inexpensive.

Like candy, not every detail needs to be pricey. It's more important to budget whatever money you do spend creatively. Sprinkle glitter, confetti, or faux jewels on plain tablecloths to add sparkling color. And, adds Dubin, "Take advantage of what is available seasonally." Go to the large discount stores to shop; in the summer you will find loads of towels, flip-flops, and candy necklaces for a beach theme. For winter, the shelves will be stocked with all the goods you need for a true wonderland, like snowflake decorations, white string lights, mittens, and more. If you time your spree well, some of your items will even be on sale, advises Dubin. The one thing you should splurge on is chairs. "It is money well spent," she says. You can leave them plain or embellish them in a number of ways; either way the result will be much more fetching than a plain old chair.

Photographs

Photography for an event like this is often thought of as an after-the-party detail in proofs and albums. But photography can also be used at the party to create an atmosphere and set the stage. Photographers can blow up prints of your child to make posters to hang around the room. The prints can be left in their original state or enhanced with color, lighting, and other special effects to transform your child's image. Photographs of other people, places, and things can also be manipulated to work into any decorating scheme. Smaller photos can be set on tables, clipped to boards, or suspended from ropes for a more subtle decorating idea. A picture of your child can even be enlarged, set on an easel and used as a sign-in board, which can hang on a wall or in her room long after the party is over. Use a baby picture, a current photo, or

even one with your child dressed just for the occasion. (FOR MORE ON PHOTOGRAPHY, SEE CHAPTER EIGHT, GETTING THE PICTURE)

Making the Most of the Space

The fact is, even the best space, unless it is totally bare (which raises other issues), may not mesh with your decorating scheme. There's no need to despair though, if the drapery is too fussy, the carpet has a busy pattern, or the walls are the wrong color. All can be remedied. Fabric can cover windows to hide unsightly views. Drapes, floors, and rugs that match your vision perfectly can be brought in to temporarily hide what's there. Even fake walls can be constructed and painted and put up just for the day. "You can do so much with fabric and props [from prop houses] to transform a space," says Polly Onet of Ober, Onet & Associates in New York City. "Party designers can come up with great ideas. They do the research and have access to the workshops, fabrics, and lighting to bring them to fruition." Of course, any of these services go in the "extra" column of the budget worksheet and depending on the work that needs to be done can cost a significant amount.

You might want to consider what is already in the space and how you can use it well. A wild carpet might stand out against the white tablecloths that covered the tables when you went to view the space. Try to pick up a color in the carpet for tablecloths you bring in. This way the carpet will blend in. The same can be said for overdone drapes or blank walls. Try to work with rather than fight them. Match drapes to other decorative elements or find out if you can have them removed or at least tied tightly back so the effect is minimal. And look at blank walls as a blank canvas you can do anything you like with. Cover with oversized photos, a simple and colorful length of a fabric banner, or have one of the vendors set up shop against the offending wall to hide any imperfections. You have to find a place, after all, for a bandstand, video-montage wall, or a projection screen (SEE CHAPTER EIGHT, GETTING THE PICTURE). And remember to focus on all the tables and seating arrangements. If done right, the effect will ripple across the room and any unfavorable sights will fade into the background.

Lighting Effects

The right lighting is also integral to the overall appearance of the room. If the lighting in your space is too bright, too white, too dim, or too yellow, there are lighting experts who can fix that. An added expense for sure, but one that most experts agree is important to include in your budget if you can. "A good lighting person is very important," says Handy, especially when a space is not ideal. These experts can hide imperfections, light a room a certain color to coordinate with your theme, and darken bad draperies so they fall into the shadows. Dubin even uses lighting effects for decorative detail purposes. For example, when she planned an event for a family who likes to boat, she had the white rectangular tables lit from the bottom with blue lights, then draped them with white cloths to create a sense of water and waves.

The Theme of the Day

Simply put, attending bar and bat mitzvah parties week after week can get a bit tedious for both the guests and the guest of honor, especially if everyone can expect the same sort of fanfare at each. One way to make your child's celebration unique is to think of a theme that is tailor-made to fit his interests and personality, and plan the party around that. Details may be woven through the whole event from decorations to favors and music to entertainment or just sprinkled here and there in a centerpiece idea or an activity. Themes are a great way to give the party a focus, to organize it, and to truly make it about your child.

Picking a Theme

Even if your child is taking a backseat in the planning details, this is one decision he should be in on. After all, a theme should be based on something your child likes, identifies with, and can get excited about. So plan some time early on to brainstorm together. You and your child

theme ideas

Any interest or inkling can be transformed into a theme. Below, a few suggestions to get you thinking.

Art **Ballet** Beach Books **Broadway** Caribbean Cooking and Baking Cars Casino **Colors** Comedy Computers Decades ('60s, '70s, '80s) **Favorite characters** Fashion Fiesta Hollywood **Judaism** Jungle Magic Movies **New York** Nightclub Rock and Roll School Science Space Sports Travel **Wall Street**

COOKIE STARTERS

Cookies mono-
grammed with the bar
mitzvah boy's initials
can be color coordi-
nated to the theme of
the day. Set at each
guest's place, they can
be sampled now or
saved for later.

can collaborate on the theme, says Onet. "Everyone has ideas and it's fun to see the different components come together." If your child plays a particular sport or is involved with a certain activity, consider that. The possibilities are endless for centerpiece and decorating ideas, entertainment, games, and favors. So even if your child's best buddy likes baseball too, not a problem. The results can be completely different. A theme can be as simple as your child's favorite color. And if you are having trouble coming up with a theme, Dubin suggests making the child the theme. Put a spin on the name for an event slogan like "Jazz It Up with Jake" or "Come Celebrate with Samantha" and decorate with poster-size photos of your child, let his or her favorite color influence the decoration, and use his or her initials to make a monogram for details from invitations to cookie decorations. You can do the same if you are having trouble narrowing down all your child's favorite ideas or activities; make your child the theme and all the things she loves to do part of the plans.

Putting a Theme in Place

Any or all of the elements for a party can coordinate with a theme. The more details you tie in, the better the effect will be. Decorations play a big part in getting the point across. Menu selections are also a fun way to keep the theme going and many caterers are happy to be creative with dishes as well as presentation.

Entertainment plays a big role too. Certainly music can set the mood as can motivational dancers, who go hand in hand with the music and can dress the part. Additional activities can also keep the party's theme strong (SEE CHAPTER SEVEN, THAT'S ENTERTAINMENT). Favors, whether goodies given at the start of the event to use during the celebration or at the end to take home, work well too. There can be, however, too much of a good thing, so it is important to think about how well all the pieces work together. Consider all your options and select the ones with the most impact. Otherwise not only will you spend more than necessary, but you will also end up with a theme that overwhelms the party rather than one that ties it all together.

Favors

As with any birthday party, it is customary for people to bring presents for the guest of honor. Bar mitzvah children have also come to like the idea of giving their guests—mostly the kids—a cool gift too. These party favors can be personalized with your child's name, the bar mitzvah date, the theme, or even your guests' names. While they are not necessary, done right, they are a wonderful keepsake. They can be small, big, inexpensive, over-the-top, or anywhere in between. Favors may be simple parting gifts or a whole lot more. Some people use them to decorate place settings—a decadent piece of

Ro led towels for a
beach-theme party are
secured with string
and stacked for guests
to take on their way
out. Tiny tins, topped
with starfish, and scat-
tered silver dollars add
to the sandy day.

favor ideas

Giving guests gifts to take home is not necessary, but it is fun for
them and you. Be as creative or as sensible as you like. Personalize
them or leave them plain. Here are some suggestions to get you
thinking. The possibilities are really endless.

Baseball hats **Beach gear** Belts with
initialed buckles Blankets Books and
bookmarks **Boxer shorts** CDs and cases
Decks of cards Disposable cameras
Duffel bags Candy Glow-in-the-dark
gear Hair barrettes and bows **Handbags**
Handmade soaps Key chains
Makeup kits **Mugs** Pens Photo
albums Picture frames Pillows
PJs Puzzles Robes **Sports
bottles** Stadium cushions Sweatshirts
T-shirts Yo-yos

For a winter celebration,
why not send guests
home with a cozy pres-
ent? This cocoa kit
comes with a mug, hot
cocoa mix, a spoon, and
gourmet marshmallows.

candy in a tiny box—or as an element of the party—blue
tie-dye socks at a blue-themed party to hand out when
kids take off their shoes for dancing. Other people hire
side entertainment (SEE CHAPTER SEVEN, THAT'S ENTER-
TAINMENT) that generates prizes and gifts. The only point
to be sure of is that everyone has a chance to participate.
This means if you have an artist airbrushing shirts, there
needs to be enough time for everyone to get one if they
like. You will want to have favors for all of the kids; you
don't necessarily need them for the adults. But remember too, that "adults get a kick out of some of this stuff
just as much as the kids do," says Onet.

Favors are more than just fun for guests, they can be a
tool for your party too. Tie them in with a theme. Or turn
end-of-the-event favors into another decorating detail:
Think about the wrapping, whether it's special boxes,
bags, paper, or cellophane. Colors for ribbons and the
wrapping itself can match the theme as can materials and
props. "For a party with a movie theme," says Onet, "we
put favors in boxes that were replicas of old movie reel
boxes." Presentation is important too. You can use big galvanized buckets for a beach theme, bags suspended from
trees for a jungle party, or decoratively wrapped favors on
a table to create a colorful display. Use cellophane bags,
pretty paper ones, tiny burlap sacks, boxes, buckets, or
trays. Tie with ribbons and label with tags. Use a rubber
stamp to embellish the tags with the bar mitzvah child's
name or initial (these can be storebought or custom-
made). Or create a message on your home computer, print
on cardstock and cut into strip tags as long as you need.
You can also set a card on the table printed with a clever
send off message and instructions for guests to please take
one. Whatever favor you choose will make a wonderful
keepsake of this very special occasion.

FAVOR BOXES

Clever containers make
taking home favors all
the more fun. And what
better boxes than "take
home" variety fancied
by Chinese restaurants.
The boxes are readily
available in a variety of
colors.

7

THAT'S ENTERTAINMENT

The music and entertainment are key factors at any celebration. They set the tempo, direct the flow, give the party energy, and make it interesting and memorable. Like any element of the bar mitzvah, the entertainment should be a reflection of your child, his interests, and his personality. It should also appeal to both kids and adults alike. Tricky to orchestrate, to be sure, but actually quite easily done once you settle on the right mix of activity, timing, and communication. There are so many choices in entertainment today, it is a bit confusing to know just what you need and where to find them. You can look for all the performers individually, meet with each one yourself, and coordinate all the various schedules. Or, you can meet with an entertainment company whose specialty it is to match the right performers and activities to you as well as direct the flow of the event. They have a slew of options and work with people of varying talents and vendors who have proven to be reliable and great successes. Some companies have set packages to choose from, others will tailor-make your occasion to fit your child's desires.

FUN FOR ALL

Dice, cards, poker chips, balls, photos, glow-in-the-dark jewelry, and more are prizes, trinkets, and tools of play for side entertainment at your celebration..

At the first meeting with an entertainment company, come prepared to share a vision for the day. Your child should come along too. Says Matt Toubin, Sales Director for Total Entertainment in Englewood, NJ, "The first step is to get a general sense of family dynamic. An understanding of the child's personality is a huge part of how to choose the right entertainment." Nobody expects you to pick exactly what you want at first, but any information you provide can give the professionals an indication of what will work well. Then they can steer you in the right direction.

In addition to a vision for the day, it's often beneficial to go in with a rough estimate of the guest list, including the number of kids and grown-ups. Any theme is helpful to share as is the location of the party. Also give a general sense of style; are you looking for fun and exciting or low-key and formal? There is no need to get too stuck on details yet. "If someone says 'I need fun, lively, and memorable,'" says Michael Cerbelli, Creative Director of Total Entertainment "that person is probably going to have the best party because he or she will be laid back and go with the flow. The people who are too focused on the details in terms of timing and party flow will be very stressed out during the event."

It is also helpful to tell entertainment companies what you don't want, such as certain music styles, particular activities, or performers—it is much easier to exclude things from the start rather than to know what to include. Almost every party has an element of music and dancing, since it is something everybody can do at once. If your venue doesn't lend itself to that or if you or your child really do not want dancing, now is the time to let the professional know so you can create a party where it won't be missed.

If you will have some degree of music and dancing, there's a lot you need to know. Here, some information to help you decipher what you may like, what you may not, and what it is all just about.

Dance Floor Entertainment

Just like it sounds, this kind of entertainment is focused around the dance floor and dancing and features the deejay or band, the emcee, and the motivational dancers. The decision of deejay versus band is not based on any formula, but strictly a matter of personal preference.

Band

Bands may be big or small, comprised of a variety of instruments or just a select few, have a vocalist or not, or play one specific style of music or be able to belt out all the popular tunes. The basic band is made up of four to six musicians. Typically there will be a keyboard player, a lead and bass guitarist, a drummer, and maybe one saxophone or trumpet player, as well as a vocalist. You can

TENNIS THEME

To create a theme for
your child's party, look
to his hobbies for
ideas. Any sport can
lend all sorts of inspiration for activities, decorations, and favors.

always add more pieces, even more vocalists. Of course, remember that the more you add on, the higher the price.

Many people think the cost is well worth it. Bands bring an element of live entertainment to the party that even the best deejay can't provide. But with bands, you won't get the songs exactly as you know and like them. Instead, you'll hear the band's version of the song, which may sound so similar to the original that you won't be able to tell the difference, or if it sounds just a little off, it might be equally fun to listen to—or not. Go check a band out at a live performance before booking them. Find out when they will be playing and if it is okay to stop by. If possible, see them perform at a venue similar to your reception site, if not at your reception site, to get a true sense of the acoustics.

Deejay

These guys and girls are really a one-stop shop when it comes to music. While some specialize in a certain music style, most have libraries with every imaginable genre and an ability to turn out just the right mix to make both kids and adults happy, or they can focus on a particular type of music if that is your wish. While bands may or may not be willing to learn a song they are not familiar with, deejays have more flexibility when it comes to special requests, simply adding CDs to their likely already vast collection. And with a deejay, you know just what

you are getting: the song you know, by the artist and musicians you know, just the way you like it.

Emcee

This person will guide the party, making one moment flow right into the next. "A great emcee allows the guests to be the stars," says Tom Kaufman of Tom Kaufman Entertainment Productions in New York City. "He will turn it on when necessary, but not try to be the center of attention." If you want an emcee to be a more high-profile member of the entertainment team, encouraging guest participation, getting to know the crowd, and letting them get to know him, you should tell the entertainment company so they find the right person. Emcees also work hand in hand with bands and deejays; musicians will often take clues from the emcee when choosing what to play next, to make the dance floor the most fun and happening place it can be.

Motivational Dancers

These professional dancers help guests to get up and moving. Without them, thirteen-year-old guys and girls might be too shy to hit the dance floor. But with these dancers—usually young, good-looking, and bursting with energy—coaxing them out of their seats and bounding around the floor, the kids can't help but want to get involved. "When you see people enjoying them-

selves, it's contagious," say Greg Telleri and David Sharky, owners of Untouchable Events in New York City. Even adults can't resist the charge from this "pep squad" and are eager to join the crowd. If you like, ask the emcee to instruct dancers to focus on both kids and single adults who are looking for a partner.

"The better the dancers, and the more they smile and exude energy, the more the people want to come to the dance floor," notes Kaufman. So it is important not to hire just any dancers. Make sure you see who you are getting for your event. Discuss any thematic costume ideas with the entertainment company before the event. Dancers usually come dressed in snug-fitting pants (good for dancing) and colored T-shirts so they easily stand out in a crowd. But most are willing to sport costumes or other outfits that work with a particular theme or color scheme.

While these dancers definitely do motivate the crowd, you don't want it to feel like they have taken over the dance floor. Cerbelli recommends using a formula: "For an average party you want one dancer for every twelve to fifteen kids, split evenly for guys and girls so that it is a nice flow on the dance floor. But if you have a very big party, you don't want it to get out of control, so max out performers at six." Dancers take their direction from the emcee, but are in sync with each other and the deejay or band at the most successful parties.

Side Entertainment

It used to be that music at a party was enough. While music is still the primary entertainment, parties today often have that and then some. Side entertainment, as it has come to be known, encompasses all other entertainment and activities away from the dance floor. It can take place throughout the entire event, for just one period of time, or open and close at various times during the event. It needs to be coordinated with other elements of the party including music, candlelighting, food service, and the cocktail hour so that guests have a chance to be at the right place at the right time without any distractions. Entertainment companies strongly recommend an entertainment coordinator be on-site at the party to ensure all of the parts are working together. If not, it is the emcee's responsibility to make sure this happens. Usually the side entertainment is geared to the kids, but adults can join in too. Before signing on any entertainment, find out if your venue allows it, has enough room, and the required electrical capacity.

Side entertainment can coordinate with a theme, or a special interest, or be creative, unique, or just something fun. There are performers and arcade games, both traditional and virtual reality 3-D types, tasty treats, strolling live talent, casino games, photo items, craft booths, multimedia options, and more (FOR SPECIFIC

BAUBLES AND
BEADS
Jewelry-making
stations, especially
fanciful beading spots,
are all the rage with
girls –and they get to
take home their goods.

IDEAS, SEE "SIDE ENTERTAINMENT," PAGE 128). Any of these performers or activities come at an extra cost. Again, you will want to figure that into the overall budget when planning. There is no need to book side entertainment until three to six months before the party date, especially if your bar mitzvah is scheduled later in the school year—your son and his friends might have seen the same entertainment fifty times during the year. Why not try something different? The exception to that rule is exclusive entertainers who are often booked a year or more in advance for their specialties.

Some of the most successful side entertainment ideas are any relating to photography. "People are already dressed up at bar mitzvahs," says Cerbelli. "They like to get their picture taken to bring home." Photos can be formal portraits, from old-time photo booths, and images superimposed on anything from T-shirts to faux magazine covers and movie posters. Families and groups of friends will often get in shots together which is lots of fun and makes lines move quickly. Any activity related to a theme works well too, like a sports arcade for a sports theme and a casino setup for a nightclub. Crafts are always a hit with both kids and adults; everyone likes to walk away with something they have created or that has been made for them. Strolling entertainment allows personalized attention from the entertainer and means that guests don't wait in lines at a station or booth for their turn. There is even the idea of making side entertainment the dance floor entertainment of the moment. "Have a specialized band perform to give a flavor to the party, so it's not the same footprint as every dance band," suggests Kaufman. You can do a '60s thing, try out a Brazilian samba band to turn the room upside down, or bring in belly dancers to throw the taste of Morocco into the mix. Reggae, Latin, and swing are popular with crowds too; they can play for half an hour—it's a quick and fun break from the regular bands, which will be gone just long enough to be missed.

Making It Work Together

Where to start? "Music is the heart and soul of the party. It's where people have fun and interact," says Kaufman. "And it's essential to capture the excitement of the night. The opening set establishes the tone for the whole party." Selecting just the right songs that kids will dance to and adults can stand to hear (and vice versa) can get pretty contentious. Take heart, though, there are plenty of ways to get it right.

The music must be eclectic, say Telleri and Sharky. No one should feel that it is one-sided. You and your child should give "play" and "don't play" lists to the band or deejay. This way, they can play a set for the kids, then one for the adults. You may also find, somewhat surprisingly, that there is a crossover in music style and

taste. So many of the adults' favorite songs and others they know well are being remade into funky and kid-friendly tunes, says Toubin. And kids hear plenty of their parents' songs in movies, on TV shows, and in commercials, and have become familiar with the originals, the remixes, and remakes; parents are also in tune to kids' songs from the car radio. So today there is less of a gap between the musical tastes of kids and adults than there once was. As for the third generation of grandparents, and great-aunts and -uncles who will be in attendance, be sure to request a few songs for them, but know many of them will like to sit back and watch everyone else with pride and enjoyment. Just be sure to seat them far enough away from direct dance floor action and the pulsating speakers.

Timing the Entertainment

Even with all the music appreciation between the older and younger guests, it is still not realistic to expect them on the dance floor all together all the time. And that's okay. The party will last awhile and everyone will get a turn. Plus there may be so much more to do, starting with the cocktail hour. "Everybody's favorite part of the night is cocktail hour," says Cerbelli. He suggests doing an extended cocktail hour because adults like to socialize and kids can get right into activities: Adults can nibble on good food and loosen up before they come into the room.

It is the perfect time to set up kids' activities so they are supervised and entertained from the start. Cerbelli also says that the bulk of the side entertainment should happen during the cocktail hour. Otherwise everyone will spend their time there and not on the dance floor. Once it is time for the party to begin, you need everyone in the room and focused on that, says Toubin. "You want to close down the activities at the beginning, and then quietly reopen them later." This takes good communication between the emcee and the entertainment coordinator. Activities and entertainers should be flexible at other times so the emcee and entertainment coordinator can close them quickly if necessary—during candlelighting, food service, video loops and montages, or when they need everyone back boogying on the dance floor. "Whatever side entertainment you have should complement, not compete with, the music," suggests Toubin.

Dancing and Then Some

You can plan multiple activities at once. They don't have to be related, but should work together in terms of space and electrical constraints, time issues, and lines. And there can be too much of a fun thing. "You want the party to gel," says Kaufman. "It won't if there is so much going on that your guests can't participate in it all." Also, the more you have, the less special it seems. So instead of feeling like you need so much or giving in to your child's desire to showcase everything, it's best to be picky and choose just one or even a select few that will work best. In the end, everyone will enjoy them more and you will be glad you did.

Sometimes that means choosing the best entertainment for your budget. Most entertainment companies agree, music is the key element of any [dance] party. And if you have to crunch numbers even more, then use this guide from Telleri and Sharky to rank the dance floor entertainment in order of must-haves. First, they say, is the deejay, then the emcee. And with just these two professionals, the party is well on its way to amazing. The dancers are next on the list, and to Telleri and Sharky, key elements of entertainment if you can square them in the budget. Then come other entertainers, crafts, and games. But, says Cerbelli, "even if you have not budgeted for extra entertainment, music and dance floor performers should provide all the makings of a fabulous event. A good emcee is there to work and to run the event and he and the performers should work their tails off for you."

Working with Entertainers

All the professionals for the event's entertainment will be under contract whether they are solo professionals or part of an entertainment company. As with every other facet of the planning process, make sure to read the contract carefully before you sign it and that you understand all the fine points that you're agreeing to. The contract needs to state when each person or group of people will arrive, how long they are expected to stay, how they factor setup and breakdown into their timeframe, and so on. Also included in the contract should be fees, overtime charges, any travel expenses, and rental fees for extra equipment. Be sure the contract stipulates how many giveaway items—for instance, glow-in-the-dark pieces, hats, sunglasses, Hawaiian leis—are included in the cost and if there is a limit on the number of guests they will cater to. The contract should spell out the attire—whether formal, casual, or specific costume. And you will also want noted how many breaks during the evening all will get (particularly dance floor entertainers) and if you need to serve them a meal (speak to the caterer about vendor meals, which are less pricey than your guests' plates).

No matter your budget or what entertainment you choose in the end, there needs to be a good team of people behind it. This group of people, whether related or not, need to be professionals who know what is expected of them, whom they need to look to for directions, and how to change the schedule on the fly. "When everyone is in sync and the team effort is in place, you will have the most successful event ever," promises Cerbelli.

side
entertainment

There is a wealth of talent and fun things to do out there and they have found their way into **parties and events** all over. Most entertainment companies will be able to provide you with a list to choose from. This list from Total Entertainment in Englewood, NJ provides an amazing variety of the **hottest entertainment** when you want to do a little bit extra.

Virtual Sports Baseball Race Cars Bike Hang Glider Kayak Rides Paintball Arcade Simulators Alpine Ski Race ATV Racing Boxing Dance Competition Guitar Competition River Rapids Shooting Gallery Soccer Classic Arcade Games Basketball Football Toss Foosball Dome Hockey Air Hockey Putting Challenge Nascar Racing Pool Table Soccer Carnivals Dunk Tank Gold Fish Racing Hermit Crab Racing Miniature Golf Nascar Race Track Bungee Cord Games Bouncy Boxing Giant Slide Giant Twister Game Gladiator Joust Human Bowling Moon Walks Obstacle Course Velcro Wall Fun Foods Candy Wall Chocolate Fountain Dippin Dots Food Truck M&M Wall Egg Cream Stand Newsstand Peanut Stand Pretzel Stand Old Time Candy Girls Popcorn Cotton Candy Snow Cones Taffy

Live Talent The World's Fastest Painter Break Dancing Show Candyman Caricaturist Celebrity Look-a-Likes Fortune Teller Handwriting Analysis Human Statues Live Musicians Magicians Mentalist Money Sculptors Mr. Trivia Robot Sixty-Second Novelist Tattoo Artist Yo-Yo Artist Theme Ideas Dance Cages Lounge Furniture Paparazzi Photo Options Coney Island Photo Booth Digital Photo Shop Hair Styling Machine Crafts Airbrush Artist Aroma Candle Art Attitude Hats CD Recording Booth Charm Jewelry Chinese Flower Painting Create a Bear DMV Station Glass Blower Jell Candles Jewelry Making License Plates Lip Gloss Pipe Cleaner Creations Sandal Art Sign Shop T-shirts Wax Handprints Wire Sculptures Multimedia Plasma TVs Video Screens Video Wall MTV Music Video Casino Black Jack Poker Roulette Texas Hold 'Em

8

GETTING THE PICTURE

The photographs and video of your child's bar mitzvah are the tiny treasures of the day. They are the pieces that will take moments in time—some you'll remember and some you won't—and transform them into wonderful and lasting memories. Put in an album or set to music on a video or DVD, they tell the story of the celebration over and over again. Then there are the photographs and films of your child that can play a big part in the decorations, activity, and spirit of the party. The photographer in charge of capturing the new shots and remaking the old ones has a quite a big job indeed, and choosing the right one can be an equally challenging task for you.

Meeting Photographers and Videographers

The first step, as is true for selecting any professional, is getting recommendations and referrals from family and friends. You want to inquire about a photographer's or videographer's style of work, to see if it is in keeping with your own ideas, and find out if he can give you the final product you are looking for. With photographers, there will be a lot of personal interaction and you want to feel comfortable with whomever you choose. So both you and your child should attend the meetings to see if you share similar ideas, thoughts, and feelings on the event.

Ask to see his portfolio and samples of work from other events he has covered. If your event will take place indoors, be sure to look at shots from indoor parties. Do the same if your celebration will be an outdoor one. Look for quality in his shots in terms of lighting; are shots too dark when taken inside or does the sun seem to get in the way of the details in photographs taken outside. Try to get a sense of the style and taste and see if it suits yours. Ask to see samples of albums the photographer has put together too, so you can see the finished product and the various choices offered. Next you need to discuss the parameters of your event, from the ceremony to the reception. Find out if the photographer has ever shot at your site before and, if not, whether he would visit to scope out potential locations for formal portraits and to figure out lighting needs. Find out how many people will work your party; it is standard to have at least two for the best coverage. You want to know if the photographer will have an assistant on hand to work the lighting equipment, change film and cameras, or if the photographer will juggle it all. For the videographer in particular, inquire about the equipment. Today, equipment is technologically advanced so that there should not be any pesky wires trailing behind or a big microphone needed to pick up well wishers' *mazel tovs*. In fact, any of these professionals should strive to be as unobtrusive as possible.

Photography Style

You want to discuss the photographer's and the videographer's style of shooting. Certainly you desire great formal shots—but to really allow your child's personality to shine through and capture the party's energy, do not limit yourself to traditional posed portraits. Instead, David Lewis Sternfeld, president of Freestyle Productions, based in New York City and Montreal, Canada, "capture the unique moments of your event by using a photojournalistic approach and set some time aside for formal shots as well." In fact, Freestyle takes it one step further. "We mix casual lifestyle shots, taken prior to the event, along with formals and unobtrusive

PHOTOGRAPHER'S
TOOLS

Documenting the
details is the photogra-
pher's job and a very
important one. He
should use more than
one camera and have
extra film and memory
cards on hand.

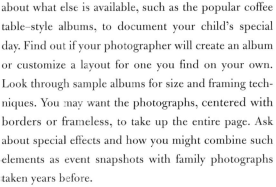

candids from the bar mitzvah," says Sternfeld. The same is true with video. Be sure your photographer and/or videographer is keen on mixing formal, candids, and documentary shots to get the best representation of the event.

The equipment used to photograph is just as important as the style. Many photographers today use both digital and traditional film to get the right combination of shots to capture the mood of the event. Bear in mind that digital and film have their advantages. When all the pictures are shot using only digital, explains Sternfeld, you lose the texture that traditional film achieves. On the other hand, you don't want to use just film and lose all the possibilities that digital technology has to offer.

The Album

Photographers typically use black-and-white film as well as color. You may want to decide with your photographer the percentage of photos to be taken in color versus black-and-white. These days you can expect more than just the classic album variety. Certainly traditional albums work well, but talk to your photographer

about what else is available, such as the popular coffee table–style albums, to document your child's special day. Find out if your photographer will create an album or customize a layout for one you find on your own. Look through sample albums for size and framing techniques. You may want the photographs, centered with borders or frameless, to take up the entire page. Ask about special effects and how you might combine such elements as event snapshots with family photographs taken years before.

Beyond the Album

Today, photographers and videographers can add to the party itself instead of simply recording the event. With new technologies, creativity, and ingenuity, photographs and videos can add to your celebration from start to finish.

Embellish invitations with photographs to add a personal touch to the festivities early on. Take formal shots especially for this purpose or find an old favorite picture. You can even have a photograph taken to match the theme of the party. Attach photos to the stationery, cover them with vellum, have them printed on, and make them color, black-and-white, or even sepia-toned. Use one photo or many in a collage or on multiple pages of an invitation booklet. Whenever a detail needs to be coordinated between two professionals, in this case the

FILM STRIPS

Contact sheets are a
photographer's tool
for viewing their work
after film develop-
ment. A few rows can
be set together,
enlarged, and framed
to tell a story.

stationer and the photographer, let each know what you are thinking and how to get in touch with the other. Some photographers are so creative with these special products and can even use graphics to enhance the picture and produce the entire invitation. And there is more.

Freestyle Productions actually produce an interactive CD-Rom invitation that guests can play right on their computer. The customized invitations might include information about the service, perhaps with a video clip hinting at the theme of the party, or, as Sternfeld suggests, the video could include a mini montage of the bar mitzvah child waving guests into the reception venue. CD-Rom invitations can also incorporate photographs and video highlighting the bar mitzvah child at different stages preparing for his big day. And everything can be set to music. "Finally," says Sternfeld, "guests can R.S.V.P. online. That's what makes it interactive."

Decorations made of photographs bring a realistic energy to the surroundings. Photos of kids can be enlarged to posters and banners and hung around the room, used as centerpieces, or even as a sign-in board for guests. Photos for posters can be left as is or graphically enhanced. This concept can work with a theme or a color scheme or just to make an impact. Group shots of friends are another decorating detail that is especially effective for the kids' lounge. They too can be blown up, enhanced, made black-and-white, and plastered all over the walls. As with all special items, discuss early on with your photographer what the possibilities are to ensure there is enough time to pull it all together.

Montages are favorite collections of photographs and video clips of the bar mitzvah child and friends or family members. Once known as "slide shows," these productions have graduated to become more sophisticated presentations and are likely to be viewed at different points during the event: just after the grand entrance, after the main course, before or during the candlelighting ceremony. Shows may last anywhere from three to six minutes. The photo montage or video loop may have shots from babyhood through the present, with photos from every season, at school and at camp, on holidays, and the like. There may be more than one video: the first, shown early on in the event, may feature just the bar mitzvah child; the other, run during the candlelighting as a loop, could be of the bar mitzvah child with family and friends. The montage may be displayed on a single big screen, several screens, or even a wall of plasma televisions set up like popular video music shows. The hippest photographers will set the show to cool music and add any number of special effects. Freestyle Productions montage is a film, actually made from two photo shoots—at the family's house and

at the studio—produced with a crew of professional editors, graphic artists, sound people, and even sometimes hair and makeup stylists.

Photo shoots can be scheduled in order to get shots it would not be possible to get on the day of. If you want your album to incorporate casual home shots and family time, special days need to be set aside to get them. The shots can also be used for invitations, decorations, and montages, and turned into prints for framing. Many synagogues do not allow photography during a Shabbat service so it is hard to capture some of the more poignant moments such as the bar mitzvah child on the *bimah*, reading from the Torah, or a grandparent opening the ark. Some synagogues will allow you and the photographer to stage shots beforehand in the weeks or days leading up to the bar mitzvah. "We recommend a dress rehearsal prior to the event," says Sternfeld. "Not only can the bar mitzvah child and his family do some fine tuning, we find that everyone is a lot more relaxed than they would be the day of the event."

Booking the Time

Many photographers offer a variety of packages for basic services that include the amount of hours they work, album to be made, and additional prints. This works fine for those who want a photographer to be on hand the day of, to present a number of proofs to select from, and to produce an album. Other photographers

are prepared to be available at other times, including the night before at Friday night dinner, earlier on the day of the event to take shots of the family getting ready, even the following day for brunch in the morning. Of course, you will be paying extra for the photographer's time, so if the extra coverage is necessary, factor that into your budget. And as soon as you know when you want the time, book it to guarantee the photographer will be there to record those moments.

Contract Details

For photography and videography, the contract needs to state the extent of coverage; additional times you will have appointments; the number of albums you will receive, including how many pages and photographs in each; and how many prints you will receive and the sizes of those prints. The contract also needs to cover the types of photographs, whether black-and-white or color, how many proofs you can expect to see, and a date when you will have the proofs, the albums, and prints. Specifics also need to be documented about any other services the photographer and videographer will provide, such as enlargements and framed shots for decorations at the reception, video loops or montages, and more. For each of these, make sure all fees, number of pieces, sizes, and delivery date are written in. And while each of these professionals should try to be behind the

scenes as much as possible as they work the event, that
is not always the case. Make sure the proper attire is
stated in the contract and that they are aware of it,
whether you want them in a tuxedo or Bermuda shorts
and a Hawaiian print shirt to go with a beach theme.
The more a photographer blends in with the crowd, the
easier it is for him to catch people at ease for candids.

With all this in place, trust that you and your child will
have every detail of the day captured forever in time—
and set to music or compiled into a book to mark another
chapter in a most special and remarkable life.

shot list

Photographers have standard
shots they will take to get the best coverage of the event,
but you cannot expect they will get to every detail you
hope for—unless you tell them. Help fill in the gaps and
leave nothing to chance by providing the photographer
with a list of must-have photos and which should be in
color or in black-and-white. Assign someone—a good
friend or family member or even the event planner—the
task of pointing out important people or details to the
photographer. The following are some must-have
photographs to think about:

Bar mitzvah child

○ getting ready—a boy tying his tie and looking in the mirror; a
   girl slipping on her shoes, getting buttoned-up in back, or
   putting on jewelry
○ being handed a *tallis* bag for the first time
○ on the pulpit reading from the Torah (staged if necessary)
○ close-up shots of the bar mitzvah child with each parent
○ with siblings—separately and together
○ with all the entertainment gear he has collected

Family and friends

○ immediate family shots
○ grandparents and other older relatives
○ family and friends who have traveled in for the occasion

Details and Decorations

○ a dressed Torah
○ the escort card table before it is dismantled
○ place settings before guests take their seats
○ centerpieces
○ food displays
○ the cake
○ the favor table before it is dismantled

Candids

○ professionals—caterer, wait staff, deejay—doing their thing
   behind the scenes
○ entertainers working the crowd

APPENDIX

IN THIS CHAPTER

- worksheets

- sources

- credits

Table Seating Worksheet

Figuring the right place to seat each guest is a tricky task—and one you won't likely finish on the first try. Due to last-minute responses, sticky family situations, and changing teenage friendships, you should consider seating charts a work-in-progress until almost the beginning of the bar mitzvah celebration. Ask your caterer for a diagram of table layouts. Use re-stickable notes to easily maneuver names around. Create a chart similar to the one below and place it in your planner to fill in when you have got some definite table arrangement plans. Once the seating list is final, give it to your caterer, calligrapher for escort cards, and others.

Guest name ....

Number in party .... Table number .... Seat number ....

○ Escort card completed

Vendor/Service Professional Worksheet

It is a good idea to have contact names and information well organized and easy to find. Use the chart below as a model to make your own worksheet.

Vendor/Service Professional Company Name ....

Contact Name (and position) ....

Address ....

Telephone/Fax/E-mail ....

Reception Date Contact Name/Telephone ....

Notes ....

Filling Rest Room Baskets

Even the most well-appointed facilities will benefit from a few must-have items no girl (or guy) should be without. Arrange some (or all) of the following items in a basket, galvanized bucket, or other container to set by the sinks or makeup vanity in both rest rooms. Buy the best quality items in the smallest sizes.

Girls' Room

Antiperspirant/deodorant (spray) Bandages Blotting tissue Comb and brush Cotton balls and swabs Hairspray Lotion Mouthwash Nail file Nail polish (clear) Sanitary items Sewing kit

Boys' Room

Antiperspirant/deodorant (spray) Bandages Comb Cotton swabs Mouthwash Hair gel Mints Sewing kit

SOURCES

Below is a list of experts whose advice and talents are found on the pages of this book. For additional sources in your area, get recommendations from friends, family, and other trusted professionals. To do research on the Internet, use search words such as bakers, cake design/decorating, caterers, entertainment, event decorating, event design, event planning, florists, party decorations, party favors, party planning, and party rentals.

JELLY BEAN JUBILEE
A collection of jelly beans makes a colorful display and a fun activity for party guests as they help themselves on the way out. White take-out containers make for portable packaging; tag them with a fitting send-off message.

CAKE DESIGNERS

Confetti Cakes
102 West 87th Street
New York, NY 10024
(212) 877-9580
www.confetticakes.com
Special thanks to Elisa Strauss.

Gail Watson Custom Cakes
335 West 38th Street, #11
New York, NY 10018
(212) 967-9167/(887) 867-5088
www.gailwatsoncake.com
Special thanks to Gail Watson who designed the magnificent confections on the back cover, pages 67 (cake), 109 (sugar box favor), 112, and front cover (monogram sugar cookie).

Sweet Lisa's Exquisite Cakes
3 Field Road
Greenwich (Cos Cob), CT 06807
(203) 869-9545
www.sweetlisas.com
Special thanks to Stephen Maronian.

CATERING

The City Bakery
3 West 18th Street
New York, NY 10011
(212) 366-1414
Special thanks to savory chef Ilene Rosen, who also contributed the culinary delights on pages 47 (grilled chicken and avocado burritos) and 60 (state fair food), and to Maury Rubin, pastry chef/owner, for the sweet delights on pages 69 (miniature lemon tarts with local berries) and 117 (homemade marshmallow party favors).

Laurence Craig Distinctive Celebrations
1799 Springfield Avenue
Maplewood, NJ 07040
(973) 761-0190
and New York, NY
(212) 581-1986
www.laurencecraigcatering.com
Special thanks to Laurence Craig.

CRAFTS

Viva Beads Enterprises
1249 Shermer Road
Northbrook, IL 60062
(800) 669-3994
www.vivabeads.com
Special thanks to Jill Manzara and Lori Mottlowitz who created the clay beads and designed the chic bracelets on page 125.

ENTERTAINMENT COMPANIES

Tom Kaufman Entertainment Productions
155 East 55th Street, Suite 5A
New York, NY 10022
(212) 223-0962/(212) 223-8381
www.tomkaufman.com
Special thanks to Tom Kaufman.

THANKS FOR COMING

Total Entertainment
7799 West Sheffield Avenue
Englewood, NJ 07631
(800) 783-9335/(201) 894-0055
www.totalentertainment.com
Special thanks to Matt Toubin and Michael Cerbelli.

Untouchable Events
915 Broadway, Suite 1010
New York, NY 10010
(212) 924-6299
www.untouchableevents.com
Special thanks to David Sharky and Greg Telleri.

EVENT PLANNERS

Ober, Onet & Associates
9 East 97th Street, Suite 2D
New York, NY 10029
(212) 876-6775
Palm Beach, FL
(561) 835-3501
Southampton, NY
(631) 283-1141
www.oberonet.com
Special thanks to Polly Onet.

Prudence Events
235 West 18th Street
New York, NY 10011
(212) 691-1356
www.prudencedesigns.net
(see also Florists)
Special thanks to Grayson Handy and Arturo Quintero.

Regina Evans, Inc.
88 Lexington Avenue
New York, NY 10016
(212) 689-5559
www.reginaevans.com
Special thanks to Regina Evans.

Victoria Dubin Event Planning & Design
Westchester, NY
(914) 682-8647
Special thanks to Victoria Dubin, who inspired the
colorful escort cards on page 89, and designed the
groovy kid tabletop on page 101.

FLORISTS

Michael George Flowers
5 Tudor City Place
New York, NY 10017
(212) 883-0304
www.michaelgeorgeflowers.com
Special thanks to Michael George who contributed the
wheatgrass flats on pages 100 and 101.

Prudence Designs
228 West 18th Street
New York, NY 10011
(212) 691-1541
www.prudencedesigns.net
(see also Event Planners)
Special thanks to Grayson Handy and Arturo Quintero,
who also created the colorful flower arrangements on
pages 51 and 104.

INVITATIONS AND CALLIGRAPHY

Gail Brill Design
46 Fawn Street
Saranac Lake, NY 12983
(518) 891-0182
www.gailbrilldesign.com
Special thanks to Gail Brill who provided her elegant
script style sheet shown on page 93.

Ivette Montes de Oca
New York, NY
(212) 427-2659
Special thanks to Ivette Montes de Oca who designed
the R.S.V.P., transportation, and thank-you cards and
invitation (multi-stripe borders) on pages 77 and 86.

Julie Holcomb Printers
1601 63rd Street
Emeryville, CA 94608
www.julieholcombprinters.com
(510) 654-6416
Special thanks to Julie Holcomb, who also created the
letterpress invitations on front jacket, and pages 2 and
86 (upper left and lower right).

Roni Gross Design
New York, NY
(212) 677-4157
Special thanks to Roni Gross who designed the letterpress R.S.V.P. card and invitation with decorative bellyband on pages 77 (top center) and 86.

RENTALS

Party Rental Ltd.
200 North Street
Teterboro, NJ 07608
(201) 727-4700
www.partyrentalltd.com
Special thanks to Eileen Koen and Jodi Jacobs for providing the chairs and cushions on pages 98 and 101; the plates on the front cover, pages 60, 98 (top, center, and bottom left, center, and right), 100, 101, 106, 109, and 112; the glassware on pages 60, 64, 100, and 106; the flatware on pages 60, 99, and 101; the napkins on pages 60 and 99 (bright yellow and off-white fringed), 100, 103, 106, and 112; the tablecloths on pages 99, 100, 104, 106, 112, 115, and 141; the table on page 101; and the serving trays on pages 47 and 69.

PHOTOGRAPHY AND VIDEOGRAPHY

Freestyle Productions
995 Wellington, #230
Montreal, Quebec, Canada H3C 1V3
(514) 397-9933
and New York, NY
(914) 844-7826
www.freestylephoto.com

Thirteen Candles LLC
P.O. Box 509
Purchase, NY 10577
(914) 844-7826
www.thirteencandles.com

Special thanks from David Lewis Sternfeld and Avis Gold Richards to the following individuals: We extend our gratitude to the entire Freestyle Productions team, as well as all the photographers and videographers who have worked with the company over the years. Also an extra special thanks to all of the event planners who create such beautiful affairs. And many thanks to the families who have graciously shared their bar and bat mitzvahs with us: The Lieberman family, The Stein family, The Mendel family, The Levine family, The Mann family, The Blatt family, The Reinsberg family, The Erani family, The Cowan family, The Cohenca family, The Cutler family, The Effron family, The Sweible family, and The Richards family.

And our gratitude also goes to Rabbi Robert Levine of Congregation Rodelph Shalom in New York City; Toby Berkow of Central Synagogue in New York City; Cantor Judy Greenfeld of Temple Emanuel in Beverly Hills, CA; and Rabbi Robert Tobin of The Conservative Synagogue in Westport, CT. And a special thanks to Marjorie Kuhn.

Credits for David Lewis Sternfeld's photographs
Emcee of More Than Music of New York City on front cover (center left).
Congregation Shaar Hashomayim of Montreal, Quebec, Canada on page 18 (bottom).
Central Synagogue of New York City on page 31.
Menorah, Torah and *yad* provided by Temple Emanuel-El-Beth-Sholom of Montreal, Quebec, Canada on page 34.
Torah provided by A-1 Sofrim, Inc. of New York City on page 35.
Kim Sozzi Band, (212) 576-1521, www.kim@creationmusic.com, on page 48.
Cake provided by Buttercup Bake Shop, 973 2nd Avenue, New York, NY 10022, (212) 350-4144, www.buttercupbakeshop.com, on page 70 (left).

Props for Ellen Silverman's photographs
Tallis and bag on page 19, *kiddush* cups on the front cover and pages 37 and 40 (center left and right), multi-stripe bordered R.S.V.P., transportation, and thank-you cards and invitation on pages 77 and 86, courtesy Aaron Freidus.
Yarmulke on page 19, *kiddush* cup on page 40 (top right), courtesy Jake and David Reichman.
Hebrew prayer book on page 22 (top right) and *kiddush* cup on page 40 (bottom left), courtesy Joshua Eisen.
Kiddush cup on page 40 (bottom right), blue-and-brown printed R.S.V.P., directions, escort, and thank-you cards, envelope, and invitation on pages 77 and 86, courtesy Peter Jacobs.
Tzedakah box on page 43, courtesy Jake Kuhn.
Letterpress R.S.V.P. card and invitation with decorative bellyband on pages 77 and 86, courtesy Tracey and David Zabar and children Benjamin, Daniel, Michael, William, and Maryrose.
Photograph by Ellen Silverman of her son Luca (soon-to-be bar mitzvahed) on page 121, courtesy Ellen Silverman.